# Narrative Politics

# NARRATIVE POLITICS

*Stories and Collective Action*

Frederick W. Mayer

OXFORD
UNIVERSITY PRESS

# OXFORD
UNIVERSITY PRESS

Oxford University Press is a department of the University of Oxford.
It furthers the University's objective of excellence in research, scholarship,
and education by publishing worldwide.

Oxford  New York
Auckland  Cape Town  Dar es Salaam  Hong Kong  Karachi
Kuala Lumpur  Madrid  Melbourne  Mexico City  Nairobi
New Delhi  Shanghai  Taipei  Toronto

With offices in
Argentina  Austria  Brazil  Chile  Czech Republic  France  Greece
Guatemala  Hungary  Italy  Japan  Poland  Portugal  Singapore
South Korea  Switzerland  Thailand  Turkey  Ukraine  Vietnam

Oxford is a registered trademark of Oxford University Press
in the UK and certain other countries.

Published in the United States of America by
Oxford University Press
198 Madison Avenue, New York, NY 10016

© Oxford University Press 2014

Library of Congress Cataloging-in-Publication Data
Mayer, Frederick W.
Narrative politics : stories and collective action / Frederick W. Mayer.
pages cm.
Includes bibliographical references and index.
ISBN 978-0-19-932446-0 (hardcover : alk. paper)  1. Communication in politics.
2. Narration (Rhetoric)—Political aspects.  3. Political sociology.  4. Political participation.
5. Social action—Political aspects.  I. Title.
JA85.M4446 2014
320.01'4—dc23
2013028714

9 8 7 6 5 4 3 2
Printed in the United States of America
on acid-free paper

# CONTENTS

# PREFACE

This book reflects a long intellectual journey, and as I reflect on the paths that led me here, I can see that it represents an attempt to integrate two strands of my intellectual life, a love of stories and a fascination with politics.

From a childhood obsession with Tolkien, to my weakness for television dramas and crime mysteries, to my near addiction to sports, I have always been captivated by stories. And I have long been fascinated by their powers: to capture our minds, to touch our hearts, to imagine ourselves into other lives and other worlds, and to teach about our own. Perhaps, too, as the grandson of a Holocaust victim for whom I am named and the son of a survivor, I have also long had an appreciation for narrative's darker powers.

My interest in politics also has familial roots. My maternal grandfather was one of the first generation of Progressive Era professional city managers, and I remember my pride as a very young boy sitting at his desk in Philadelphia's city hall. My mother was active in local politics and the League of Women Voters. And growing up in Atlanta of the 1960s, it was hard not to be aware of the political winds.

As an undergraduate at Harvard, I started out as a government major but soon found myself drawn to history and literature, not to "high" literature and formal history so much as to folklore, mythology, and popular narratives as active forces in human affairs. A freshman seminar introduced me to the writings of Geertz and Levi-Strauss, Northrup Frye's course on the Bible as literature had a profound influence, and historians David Donald and Bernard Bailyn were inspirations. I wrote my undergraduate thesis on the role of narratives in the Atlanta race riot of 1906, focusing on the rape narratives that suffused the popular mind of white racists and triggered the attack on black Atlanta.

In my professional career, though, politics long appeared to win out over stories. My first full-time job was at a non-profit educational organization in Washington, where I taught high school students who came to DC to learn about government. I then left for the Kennedy School of Government at Harvard, first for a master's degree and then a PhD in public policy, where the emphasis was very much on technical training. My doctoral dissertation, written under the direction of the game theorist Howard Raiffa, was an application of negotiation theory to the relationship between domestic politics and international relations.

When I arrived at Duke in 1988, my research focus was far from narrative. But early in my academic career I had an opportunity to take a sabbatical leave and join the staff of US Senator Bill Bradley, where I landed at the center of the intense political battle over the North American Free Trade Agreement (NAFTA). Thrust into the political fray, I quickly realized just how incomplete my models of politics were. What struck me as I tried to make sense of the increasingly contentious battle and to devise a strategy for passing implementing legislation was that the politics of NAFTA were driven less by economic effects than by symbolic meanings. And to understand the meaning of NAFTA, and the passions it aroused, I found myself turning back to my early training in narrative.

In the years since I have found myself more and more convinced of the centrality of stories in politics and more and more puzzled by how little attention political science, in particular, has paid to them. Storytelling is the lifeblood of politics. It is what politicians do, what organizers do, what lobbyists do, what joiners and voters and protesters do. That stories matter is not news to those who practice politics, of course. Yet the academic literature on politics lacked anything approaching a complete account of the role of stories in politics. Moreover, the extensive scholarship on collective action was largely and conspicuously silent on the role of stories, curious because it is in large-scale collective action—protests, rallies, elections, and social movements—that stories are most prominent.

It has taken me far longer than I expected to write this book. Although the seeds of my thinking were sown long ago, to do justice to the topic required an exploration of multiple relevant literatures, each of which had something to say about the role of narrative in mind and society. I found myself reading works in psychology, social movement theory, and behavioral economics; narrative theory, cultural studies, history and historiography; and evolutionary theory and neuroscience. Spinning so far afield has its dangers, but I am convinced that there is great value to truly interdisciplinary inquiry that draws not only on the disparate disciplines within the social sciences, but also on both new developments in the behavioral sciences and older insights from the humanities.

Not surprisingly, given this book's long gestation, I have many people to acknowledge. Howard Raiffa, Mark Moore, and Robert Reich were early mentors and inspirations in my graduate years at Harvard. My colleagues at the Duke Sanford School of Public Policy have provided great encouragement and helpful criticism along the way. I am particularly indebted to Phil Cook, Kristin Goss, Jay Hamilton, Judith Kelley, Anirudh Krishna, and Alex Pfaff. I am also indebted to the Franklin Humanities Institute at Duke for funding for a year-long workshop on "Narrative in Action," and to my co-convener, Anne Marie Rasmussen, a scholar of medieval German literature. The workshop brought together an extraordinary interdisciplinary group of faculty including historians Bob Korstad and Tom Robisheaux, documentary photographer Alex Harris, theologian Richard Lischer, marketing scholar Joel Huber, human rights lawyer Catherine Admay, choreographer Nancy Dickenson, musicologist Tom Brothers, and psychologist Melanie Green (an interloper from Chapel Hill). Lunch conversations with Ted Fiske pushed me to clarify my thinking. And outside of Duke, I benefitted enormously from conversations with many colleagues, most notably Marshall Ganz, Peter Katzenstein, Robert Keohane, and Laura Roselle.

My students over the years have been a great help to me. Always, they were the intended audience. And I learned a great deal by imposing early drafts on undergraduates in my "Narrative and Leadership" and "Political Analysis for Public Policy" courses, and my doctoral seminar on the "Political Economy of Public Policy."

My greatest debt, though, is to my family. My sons Paul, Michael, and David, who share my love of story, practically grew up with the book. And my wife, Mary Kay Delaney, whose own work is on the social foundations of education, was not only a perfect critic and sounding board, but also an inspiration for much of my thinking.

# Narrative Politics

# CHAPTER 1

# Introduction

*Man is in his actions and practice essentially a story-telling animal.*
Alasdair MacIntyre (1981, 201)

*I have a dream today.*
Martin Luther King Jr.

On August 28, 1963, over 200,000 people gathered at the Lincoln Memorial in Washington, DC. That afternoon, the last of a long lineup of speakers stepped to the microphone and began to tell a story. "Five score years ago..." the young preacher opened, with words that echoed the opening lines of the Gettysburg Address, perhaps the most sacred of American speeches, "a great American, in whose symbolic shadow we stand today, signed the Emancipation Proclamation.... But one hundred years later, the Negro still is not free. One hundred years later, the life of the Negro is still sadly crippled by the manacles of segregation and the chains of discrimination." He told a story of promises made and not kept, a tragedy not just for African Americans, but for all Americans. America had failed to make good on its premise that "all men, yes, black men as well as white men, are created equal" and its promise that they would be guaranteed the "unalienable Rights" of "Life, Liberty and the pursuit of Happiness." America had failed to live up to its true character.

But then his story took a dramatic turn. "Let us not wallow in the valley of despair, I say to you today, my friends. And so even though we face the difficulties of today and tomorrow, I still have a dream." With those words, the narrative pivoted from a tragic past to a triumphant dream of the future, a story of redemption and of freedom, a dream "deeply rooted in the American Dream," a dream "that one day this nation will rise up and live out the true meaning of its creed: 'We hold these truths to be self-evident: that all men are created equal,'" a dream "that one day every valley shall be exalted, every hill and mountain shall be made low, the rough places will be made plain, and the crooked places will be made straight, and the glory of the Lord shall be revealed." The story he told captured his audience and moved a nation.

Martin Luther King Jr.'s challenge that day, as it was through the whole of the civil rights movement, was a problem of collective action. He had not just to rouse those gathered before him as he spoke, but also to steel them for the days to come, to reinforce their resolve when it would be easy to walk away and let others carry the heavy load. Of course, those gathered on the Mall were predisposed to hear his message, but at the same time that he was speaking to the already enlisted, he had to reach the much larger community of Americans whose support he also needed.

Why, then, standing before the largest audience he had ever faced, knowing that television would broadcast his words to millions more, did King choose to tell a story? Why locate that story in the great stories, the core historical myths of America and the Christian Bible? Why not simply make the pragmatic, political, logical, or legal case for civil rights legislation? Why with his greatest opportunity to promote collective action did King turn to narrative? Equally important, why was his story so moving for those who had travelled from afar to stand on the Mall that day and for those who heard his words on the nightly news that evening? Why did King's words resonate so well with his audiences and echo in the American consciousness from that day to ours?

In this book I seek to answer these questions and to demonstrate why it is that whenever presidents rally a nation to face some threat, generals address their troops on the eve of battle, union leaders seek solidarity, social activists urge direct action, candidates campaign for votes, interest groups solicit contributions, preachers call their congregations to serve, or coaches challenge their players to sacrifice for the team—indeed, whenever there is a need for collective action—leaders so often tell stories. And I show that those who answer the call to action, who march into battle, who stand in solidarity, who march in protest, who campaign for their candidate, who contribute to causes, who serve their God, or who sacrifice for the team, often do so not because it is in their "interest" but because they are compelled by the dramatic imperative of a collective story in which they have come to see themselves as actors. King told a story that day in Washington because by engrossing his audience in a collective narrative, he lifted those within earshot out of the cool calculus of self-interest to a passion for social justice and had them feel the dramatic potential of the moment both in the American story and, crucially, in the story of their own lives, thus making participation in the social drama of the movement a deeply meaningful expression of personal identity.

Remarkably, scholars concerned with explaining collective action have largely ignored stories. Accounts of political behavior that dominate the leading journals of the field—whether behavior by voters, legislators, presidents, interest groups, political parties, or nations—almost always strip away the rhetoric of politics and focus instead on the interests and/ or institutions that are thought to really matter (There are some notable exceptions in political communication, social movement theory and elsewhere, which I will discuss in Chapter 3.). This is an unfortunate omission. Focusing almost to exclusion on interests and institutions—although both clearly matter—and largely ignoring stories, not only loses the color, the passion, and the drama of real politics, it also misses "the best clues about why people act as they do" (Hinchman and Hinchman 1997, xiv). Stories are not merely the surface of politics; they are its heart. And they are particularly central for the core problem of politics: the problem of collective action.

Humans are story-telling animals. When we gather at parties, when we teach our children, when we court our lovers, when we gossip at the office water cooler, when we reconnect at family and class reunions, when we recount our weekend to colleagues on Monday mornings, we tell stories. Our favorite entertainments—movies, novels, television dramas, even music and sporting events—are narratives. The nightly news and the daily paper are compilations of stories. Our religious texts are story anthologies. Stories are the air we breathe.

The implications for politics of the human impulse to think and communicate in stories—with plot and drama, heroes and villains, and all the rest—are profound. But, perhaps because narrative is so ubiquitous, like air, it is hard to see. As Hayden White has observed, "So natural is the impulse to narrate, so inevitable is the form of narrative for any report of the way things really happened, that narrativity could appear problematical only in a culture in which it was absent...." (White 1980, 5).

The lack of attention to narrative in political science is remarkable considering the extensive literature on narrative in other disciplines. Scholars in cultural anthropology and cultural studies, developmental and social psychology, sociology, history and philosophy, as well as in education, law and business, have all had much to say about the nature of narrative and its importance in human endeavors. And, of course, narrative studies are central to the humanities. Scholars of literature, art, dance, and music all recognize that narrative is somehow at the heart of what it means to be human. Yet, such are the divisions in the academy, particularly the great divide between the humanities and the social sciences, that very little of this has found its way into the study of politics.

Although others have noted the importance of narrative, in this book I break new ground by developing a narrative theory of collective action. I do so by pulling together insights from the humanities, social psychology, and cultural studies about the centrality of narrative in human thought, emotion, and behavior with those from political science, economics, and sociology about the problem of collective action. This is an ambitious exercise to be sure. By covering so much territory, I have likely done some violence to the nuances of particular lines of scholarship. But there is great virtue in truly interdisciplinary work. By stepping out of the comfort of our narrow disciplinary boundaries, we can see both the limits of our previous thinking and the possibilities for new ways of thinking.

The argument of this book proceeds in three parts. The first section deals with the problem of collective action and the ways in which scholars have sought to explain how groups overcome it. The second section involves a discussion of the extent to which we humans are storytelling animals and as such can be moved by stories told to us. And the third explores how the tool of narrative enables a community to construct a common interest in a collective good and to solve the problems of collective action in pursuit of that good.

Because it is necessary to be clear about the fundamental nature of the problem for which narrative might be the solution, I begin, in Chapter 2, by reconceptualizing the problem, or rather *problems*, of collective action. These problems can be divided into those related to collective action in pursuit of a collective good and the even more fundamental problem of constructing a common interest in some good in the first instance.

Usually, the collective action problem is defined as a failure to *cooperate* in pursuit of public goods.[1] Environmental protection, national defense, and social justice are all examples of public goods. The problem is that no matter what others do, it will always be tempting to avoid the costs of cooperating while enjoying the benefits for free, that is, getting a "free ride." The essential logic of such situations is that of the familiar prisoner's dilemma game and would seem inevitably to lead to mutual defection, a consequence of which is that the good will not be produced or achieved.

Free riding can explain a remarkable array of market, societal, and political phenomena: why markets fail to produce goods that all would desire, why social groups fail to act in ways that would make their members better off, and why politics fails to produce policies in the public interest. The same logic applies to commons goods, another form of collective good, in which the temptation to exploit can lead to overuse of a common resource.

The classic example is of a public commons for livestock, in which all have an incentive to keep adding sheep, for example, because the benefit of one more sheep is enjoyed privately while the costs of reduced grass are borne by others (Hardin 1968).

Free riding is indeed a profound problem, but it is not the only obstacle to collective action in pursuit of a collective good. In some circumstances, participating in collective action (cooperating) may be preferable to not participating (defecting), but only if there are a sufficient number of other cooperators. In such cases the problem is one of *assurance*: if we believe that others will cooperate we will too, but if we doubt, defection is a temptation. The essence of the problem can be modeled as a "stag hunt," a name that refers to Jean Jacques Rousseau's parable of a group of hunters who encircle a stag, knowing that if all stay at their post, the deer cannot escape and all will benefit. But if any abandons his spot, perhaps tempted by a rabbit running by, the deer will break free. If there is any doubt about the steadfastness of others, therefore, defection becomes a temptation.

Assurance problems are much more important in social life than their treatment in the collective action literature would suggest. The problem of institutional creation is often much better modeled as a stag hunt than a prisoner's dilemma, for example. Indeed, as Rousseau argued, assurance is what enables the basic social compact. And, as I will discuss, many apparent solutions to the prisoner's dilemma often end up merely transforming the game into a stag hunt, and, therefore, the challenge from overcoming free riding to providing assurance.

The highly stylized prisoner's dilemma and stag hunt games, however, abstract away another common problem with collective goods. In most circumstances, there will be more than one way to cooperate, and, therefore, a need to *coordinate* collective action. If the issue is where two people should meet for dinner, for example, and they care only that they meet, the problem is relatively simple to solve with minimal communication. Complex collective action involving many parties and many possibilities for cooperation poses a greater challenge, however, particularly if communication is limited. And a further difficulty arises when there are asymmetric interests with respect to outcomes: if, for example, all want to meet for dinner, but some like Italian food and others like Indian. Most political collective action requires highly complex coordinated behavior among individuals who share a common general interest in some goal, but who have different views about what form cooperation should take.

The problems of cooperation, assurance, and coordination can be formidable obstacles to collective action. Note, however, that all assume the existence of common interests. But before there can be collective action, a group must share a common interest in some end. And that is far from given. Often, therefore, the first challenge is to *construct* the collective good.

The challenge arises in part because the basis of even individual interests is generally more problematic than social scientists tend to assume. To a very great degree, once we get beyond fundamental human desires for food, shelter, power, and the like, our interests are at least partially constructed. That is certainly true for *non-egoistic* altruistic, ideological, or patriotic interests that are often the basis of collective action, since those interests must necessarily be constructed. And for a group of individuals to arrive at a common interest in a collective good is even more problematic. Somehow those interests must be commonly constructed.

Given all the challenges—overcoming free riding, providing assurance, facilitating coordination, and constructing common interests—the problem of collective action would seem nearly impossible to solve. Yet people do vote, do join interest groups, do march in protest, do contribute to political campaigns, do inform themselves about public affairs, and do otherwise engage in collective action. The puzzle is to explain how they do it.

Not surprisingly, there is a considerable literature on the topic. In Chapter 3, I survey how scholars have sought to explain collective action and recognize the insights provided by the major schools of thought. Rational choice approaches assume, as the name suggests, that individuals act rationally, that is, as if they were pursuing some set of interests. Most of this literature addresses the free rider problem, and takes one of two tacks, arguing either that individuals must receive benefits from acting cooperatively that are independent of enjoyment of the collective good itself, or that cooperation can evolve when individuals interact repeatedly. Institutional approaches fall into two camps as well: one that retains assumptions of individual rationality but focuses on how previously established laws, rules, norms, conventions, and other institutions constrain behavior to facilitate cooperation, and the other that assumes that human thought and behavior are themselves institutionalized in ways that enable collective action. Social constructivist approaches to collective action are less well represented in the literature, in large part because constructivists have tended not to recognize fully the nature of the problem. Constructivists generally argue for the importance of ideational structures, among them language, symbols, ideology, and narrative in structuring human thought and action. Those constructivists who have grappled with the collective action problem have drawn particularly on the concept of "frames," defined as "schemata of interpretation" that enable individuals "to locate, perceive, identify, and label" occurrences in the world (Goffman 1974, 21). A constructivist take on collective action argues that it is enabled by "collective action frames" that operate by "assigning meaning to and interpreting relevant events and conditions in ways that are intended to mobilize potential adherents and constituents, to garner bystander support, and to demobilize antagonists" (Snow and Benford 1988, 198).

There are many insights in these literatures, but on its own each school also has its limitations: because it starts with too narrow a definition of the problem, because it applies to only a limited domain of circumstances, or because it assumes away core aspects of the problem. Even taken together, the literature leaves a large opening for a theory that can more fully account for how communities construct common interests, make cooperation in pursuit of those interests satisfying for its members, assure each that others will participate, and script coordinated behavior–an opening for a narrative theory of collective action.

To lay the foundation for such a theory, it is necessary first to understand the extent to we humans are, as Alasdair MacIntyre (1997) has called us, "the story-telling animal." In the second section of the book, therefore, I explore the remarkable role played by stories in mind and action. I begin in Chapter 4 by defining the essential features of a story, arguing that conventions about plot, character, and causality constitute a shared code in which complex meanings can be conveyed and comprehended.[2] Because we share such a code, we know what a story is, we know what a story means, and we know how to respond to a story. I then turn to the role of narrative in mind, arguing that stories serve several important psychological functions. Stories are cognitive tools. We make sense of our world through the stories we tell about it. By placing events in the familiar code of story, we impose order on our experiences, making them appear the natural consequence of circumstance and agency. Stories are also affective triggers. Indeed, I argue, emotions and narrative are so deeply intertwined that it is hard to talk about emotion without also talking about narrative.

But the psychological role of narrative goes deeper still. Stories imbue our experience with "meaning." Events become meaningful to the extent that they can be fit into or evoke some larger narrative about ourselves or our world. Stories establish our identity. Our sense of self depends on our ability to cast ourselves as the main actor in our autobiographical narratives. It is impossible to say who we are without telling a story. And, finally, stories motivate our actions. When we act we are often to a great extent *enacting*, we are acting out the story as the script demands, acting in ways that are meaningful in the context of some story and that are true to our character's identity.

As creatures constituted by narrative, we can be called by the stories told to us by others, called to attention, called to care, and called to action. As

I explore in Chapter 5, a good story can capture our minds, engrossing us and transporting us into other worlds. In so doing, it may stir our passions, alter our beliefs, and establish our interests, including those non-egoistic interests that are often the basis of collective action. Stories about others are the basis for altruistic interests, those about ideas for ideological interests, and those about our community for patriotic interests. Moreover, some stories can pull us so far into them that we see ourselves as actors in the story, can transform us from audience to participants, casting us as characters in an unfolding drama. When this happens, our character is at stake in the drama, and our identity requires that we do what the plot demands, do what is right, do what is moral.

The third section of the book then brings together the first two to show how shared narratives enable collective action. In Chapter 6, I argue that narrative can solve the problem of constructing a collective good. Stories are shared; indeed, they are primarily meant to be shared, and for that reason they can be held at once in many minds. Through shared narratives, a community can not only come to recognize its common self-regarding (egoistic) interests in such matters as security or protecting the commons, but can also construct common altruistic interests in the fate of others, common ideological interests in the fate of ideas, and common patriotic interests in the fate of the community itself.

The sociological functions of shared narratives in culture recapitulate the psychological functions of narrative in mind. To the extent that a number of individuals have the same stories in mind, it becomes possible to say that the community remembers, believes, feels, and desires. As individually held narratives construct schemas in mind, so shared narratives establish a community's basic orientation, its worldview and values, and its collective interest. Not all stories work, of course. Many factors will affect whether a story captures the mind of a community, among them who is privileged to tell the story and whether a story reinforces self-interests. But stories that work are also those that resonate with the stories a community already holds in mind, the religious, historical, political, and popular mythologies of culture. The shared narratives of culture constitute the initial stock of plot forms, character types, and meanings available to those who would weave new narratives and persuade a community of its common interest in a collective good.

Finally, in Chapter 7, I return to the puzzle of collective action in pursuit of a collective good to show why it is that narrative is the essential human tool for solving the three issues of free riding, assurance, and coordination.

First, by making participation in collective action an essential expression of personal identity, narrative can solve the free rider problem.

When individuals are transported by a collective story and come to see themselves as actors in it, their involvement in the social drama can become a pivotal vignette in their autobiographical narrative. That is why those who would move a community to collective action seek to engross their audiences in a common narrative in which the present moment is cast as the potential turning point that will turn tragedy into triumph, in which the outcome depends on collective action, and in which, for each individual, the choice of whether to participate in that action has meaning in their own life story.

Second, for complex forms of collective action, shared narratives can coordinate cooperation, enabling members of a community to imagine how they should behave and defining the form cooperation should take. Social dramas are a form of cultural convention that establish what roles are to be played and how. That is why Americans march on Washington or form a "Tea Party," the French erect barricades, the faithful go on pilgrimages, and so on. Because each knows how others will act, it becomes possible to act collectively.

Finally, narrative can solve the problem of assurance. Assurance depends ultimately on the credibility of commitment. Will you do what you say you will do, and will I? By framing cooperation as the dramatic imperative of our autobiographical narrative, we commit ourselves to cooperate. Because we can stake our character, our reputation, our life story as collateral, we can assure others that we will cooperate. And because we believe that others, like ourselves, are creatures of narrative, and believe that they too can be held to account by the stories in which they are also engrossed, we are assured that they, too, will stay in character, will do the right thing, the moral thing. That is why we so often see demonstrations of mutual engrossment in collective narrative in the moments before collective action, on the field of the impending battle, at the political rally, and in the locker room. By observing the emotional response of the community caught up in the collective drama, we are assured that all under its spell will be held to their promises.

Our biological capacity for narrative may well have evolved because it provided such a powerful and flexible tool for collective action. There is considerable evidence that human narrativity developed in concert with the rise of more complex civilizations requiring more complex forms of collective action. This would seem no coincidence. Of course, collective action is possible without narrative. Bees do quite well without telling stories. But a species that can imagine its circumstance, spin a story that alerts it to its common problem, and use that story to spark a collective response would have great advantages over one that did not.

The great gift of narrative is not always benign. The same tool that King used so masterfully to move a nation to overcome the evils of segregation was used by Hitler to enlist the German people in the evil collective action of Nazism. We can be called by false prophets as well as true. Like all powerful tools, narrative is dangerous. And for that reason, in our time, it is all the more important to understand the power of narrative and to use it with care and humility as we seek collective responses to the challenges that confront us.

PART ONE

*Collective Action*

# CHAPTER 2

# The Problems of Collective Action

*[T]hey devote a very small fraction of time to the consideration of any public object, most of it to the prosecution of their own objects. Meanwhile each fancies that no harm will come to his neglect, that it is the business of somebody else to look after this or that for him; and so, by the same notion being entertained by all separately, the common cause imperceptibly decays.*
Thucydides (Thucydides and Crawley 1933)

*If it was a matter of hunting a deer, everyone well realized that he must remain faithful to his post; but if a hare happened to pass within reach of one of them, we cannot doubt that he would have gone off in pursuit of it without a scruple.*
Jean-Jacques Rousseau (Rousseau 1997)

The problem of collective action is perhaps *the* central problem of social life. In innumerable circumstances, in business, in families, in sports, and in politics, indeed in virtually every aspect of life, coordinated collective action can lead to better outcomes than uncoordinated individual action. Yet there are formidable obstacles to successful collective action. In this chapter I will explore the nature of the problem, or rather, problems, that conspire against collective action. My purpose is to identify the essential challenges that must be met for a community to act collectively.

The problem of collective action has not always been recognized. Aristotle seems to have missed it entirely, blithely commenting that "[m]en journey together with a view to particular advantage, and by way of providing some particular thing needed for the purposes of life, and similarly the political association seems to have come together originally, and to continue in existence, for the sake of the general advantages it brings" (quoted in Olson 1965, 6). So, too, did the pluralistic school of thought that dominated American political science in the mid-20th century, which treated politics as a contest among pressure groups whose influence was largely a function of their size (Olson 1965).

On the other hand, other social observers have long grasped the essence of the matter. Thomas Hobbes placed the problem at the center of his philosophy, viewing the impossibility of voluntary cooperation as the reason why life in the state of nature was "solitary, poor, nasty, brutish and short" (Hobbes 1894, 64). In the absence of the Leviathan, he maintained, individuals would not cooperate to advance their collective interests: "Without a common power to keep them all in awe, [men] are in that condition which is called warre" (Hobbes 1894, 83).

The contemporary literature on the collective action problem derives from the theory of games, first developed by John von Neumann and Oskar Morgenstern (1944), and the economic concept of public goods, first formalized by Paul Samuelson (1954). These ideas were then the basis for Mancur Olson's seminal work, *The Logic of Collective Action* (Olson 1965), which launched the extraordinary output of scholarship on collective action that followed. That literature is far too vast to do full justice to here, but in one form or another, the problem of collective action became the central concern of scholarship on political participation, interest groups, social movements, environmental institutions, and international relations.

Most of this literature focuses on the *cooperation* problem posed by public goods, situations in which all in a group would benefit from collective action but each is nevertheless tempted to "free ride" on the actions of others. The focus on cooperation, however, has tended to obscure two other obstacles to collective action. A second potential problem is that of *assurance*, which arises whenever individuals might actually prefer to cooperate but only if others cooperate as well, a far more pervasive problem than originally credited by the literature. Yet a third common obstacle is the problem of *coordination* that arises whenever there is more than one way to cooperate and, therefore, ambiguity about which cooperative solution to adopt. These three challenges—cooperation, assurance, and coordination—can be thought of as constituting the collective action problem *given* common interests in some end—that is, given a collective good.

But largely ignored in the collective action literature is perhaps an even more fundamental obstacle confronting those who would move a community to act collectively: the construction of a common interest in some end. As I will discuss below, public goods often need to be constructed, either because members of a group lack understanding of how some outcome might affect their interests, or, more profoundly, because interests themselves must be constructed.

## COLLECTIVE GOODS, SOCIAL DILEMMAS, AND FREE RIDING

A problem of cooperation arises in the presence of *public goods*, which have the twin properties of non-excludability—if provided for one they are provided for all—and non-rivalry—consumption by one does not diminish consumption by others (Samuelson 1954). Classic examples are national defense and lighthouses. The problem is that if all who benefit from such goods choose whether or not to cooperate solely on the basis of a calculation as to whether the benefits of cooperating outweigh the costs, none will be willing voluntarily to pay for such goods, since each could enjoy the benefits without paying, and therefore all have an incentive to shirk or "free ride" on the efforts of others.

The essence of the free rider problem posed by public goods is commonly modeled as a simple two-party "prisoner's dilemma."[1] In the now familiar classic formulation, the police have arrested two suspects in a crime, but lack evidence they would need to convict them. The police separate the prisoners for questioning. Each now faces a well-defined choice: to *cooperate* with his partner by remaining silent when questioned, or to *defect* by implicating his partner. If both cooperate by staying silent, the frustrated police can only imprison them for a short time on lesser charges. If, however, one defects (gives his partner up) while the other cooperates (stays mum), the defector gets a reward of serving no prison time, while his partner will get sent away for many years. If both defect (each implicates the other), they each get an intermediate number of years in prison.

The essential characteristics of such situations are modeled in Figure 2.1. Two parties, A and B, can each choose one of two strategies, Cooperate or Defect. Their strategic options lead to four possible outcomes (the four cells of the matrix), with payoffs to A listed first and to B second (higher numbers are better). The essential point is that no matter what the other party chooses to do, defection will give a higher payoff than cooperation. Defection is therefore a *dominant* strategy, since it always beats cooperation. Moreover, mutual defection is in *equilibrium*, because after the fact, knowing what the other party actually chose, neither party would want to change its decision. But, and this is the great appeal of the model, the outcome is collectively suboptimal, in that each could have done better if both had cooperated.

Three features of the prisoner's dilemma deserve highlighting. First, no communication is allowed between the prisoners, presumably making it more difficult to collude, that is, to commit to cooperating with each other. This restriction is interesting, since talk is cheap and shouldn't alter the situation if all the parties cared about was their numerical payout. Indeed,

## The Prisoner's Dilemma

B

| | COOPERATE | DEFECT |
|---|---|---|
| **COOPERATE** | **3,3** | **1,4** |
| | | |
| **DEFECT** | **4,1** | **2,2** |

A

Payoffs to 'A' listed first, to 'B' second. '4' is best and '1' is worst.

**Figure 2.1: The Prisoner's Dilemma**
Party A chooses row, Party B chooses column. Party A's playoffs are given first, with 4 best and 1 worst.

the necessity of preventing communication in this game suggests something about our intuition about why stories might matter, a point to which we will return. Second, the players lack any mechanism to enforce agreement between the prisoners. Indeed, their problem can be reinterpreted as essentially a commitment problem (Frank 1988); if the parties could commit to mutual cooperation, that is, could enter into a binding contract, the problem is solved. And, third, the situation is constructed as a one-time encounter, so that the choices the parties make will have no influence on future interactions.

The problem posed by public goods can be modeled as a multi-party social dilemma game that follows the same logic as the prisoners' dilemma. As in the two-party prisoner's dilemma, each player faces a choice of paying for the public good ("Cooperate") or free riding on the efforts of others ("Defect"). The game is depicted in Figure 2.2 with payoffs to one party for Cooperate and Defect (measured on the vertical axis) that depend on the percentage of other players who choose to cooperate (the horizontal axis). All players face the same choices and payoffs. Because the marginal benefit to each individual of cooperation is small relative to its cost, each player has payoffs such that no matter what others do, defection will always yield the higher payoff—in other words, defection is the dominant strategy. As in the prisoner's dilemma, the rules preclude strategic collaboration: the

## The Social Dilemma

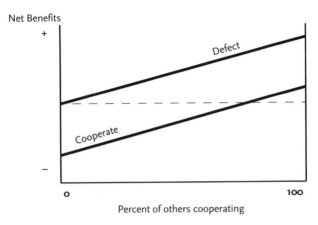

Figure 2.2: The Social Dilemma

players have no ability to contract with each other (including the ability to monitor or enforce such contracts) and play in this game has no implications for future games. If the players seek only to maximize their individual payoffs, therefore, logically all will defect even though mutual cooperation would have been better for all.

Olson distinguished between the logic of the situation with small groups (two being the smallest) and large groups, a point emphasized in Richard Tuck's recent work in which he argues that free riding is less of a concern than it has generally been taken to be (Tuck 2008). Tuck maintains that there is no free rider problem in the two-party version, drawing in part on his interpretation of Olson's distinction. Olson's point, however, was not that there was a fundamental difference in the essential logic of the social dilemma with small groups, but rather that small groups were more likely than large to deviate from the conditions specified in the social dilemma model. First, with a small group, there is a greater likelihood that the private benefits of the public good would be great enough for one party to warrant providing some amount of the good. Even then, he argued that "there is tendency in small groups toward a suboptimal provision of collective goods" (Olson 1965, 28) because even if some level is provided by the individual who benefits most, others will free ride. Second, Olson noted, when groups are small it will be easier for them to establish and enforce social norms. "[I]n general, social pressure and social incentives operate only in groups of smaller size, in the groups so small that the member can have face-to-face contact with one another" (Olson 1965, 62). If social incentives are strong enough, groups no longer face a social dilemma, of course, but the question of when such incentives arise is a good deal more complicated than Olson suggests and is by no means solely a function of group size. Although the basic logic for social dilemmas involving large and small groups is the same, therefore, as a practical matter cooperation in pursuit of public goods tends to become more difficult as groups get larger. For this reason elections and social movements face particularly acute problems, as they involve a very large number of actors. A significant implication of scale is the asymmetry between concentrated "special" interests and more diffuse general interests in society. Concentrated interests, of manufacturers in protecting their particular industry from international competition, for example, do not face a collective action problem to the same degree as general interests, of consumers in lower-priced imports, to continue the example (Schattschneider 1935).

It is worth noting that few goods are actually pure public goods. *Impure public goods* have elements of both private and public. Education, for example, often cited as a public good, is at least partly private in that it is partially excludable (the benefits of an education are largely enjoyed by those who are educated). One can think of an impure public good in terms of externalities. In the case of education, there is sufficient private benefit for a market to form, but absent intervention the good will be underprovided. Note that an institution that intervened to overcome the externality problem might have the properties of a public good. *Local public goods* involve benefits for only a subset of society, often but not necessarily in a particular locality (hence "local"). A lighthouse is only a public good for those who sail, for example, and a candidate's victory is only a public good for her supporters. *Asymmetric public goods* are those for whom the costs and/or benefits of provision are unevenly distributed because there is heterogeneity in the community. Although most public goods models assume homogeneity, in fact there are almost always differences in interests within the community. Even for the "pure" public good of national defense, for example, there may be stark differences in beliefs about how much is needed. For all three deviations from pure public goods, the free rider problem remains central, although the deviations may introduce additional complications.

The problem of cooperation illustrated by the social dilemma game also applies to the very important category of *common goods*, also referred to as *common property resources* (CPRs). Hardin's famous allegory of the "tragedy of the commons" first called attention to the issue (Hardin 1968). In Hardin's telling, farmers sharing a common unfenced pasture will inevitably overgraze it. If all would cooperate by restraining themselves to some sustainable number of livestock, the commons could be sustained. But because each individual enjoys the private benefits of grazing an additional head of sheep or cattle, while imposing the costs (in the form of less grass) on others (i.e., a negative externality), each has an incentive to defect (by grazing additional livestock) rather than to cooperate.

Common goods differ from public goods in that, although they are generally non-excludable (fish stocks are available to all, for example), use (beyond a certain point) depletes the resource and is, therefore, rivalrous. Familiar common goods are natural endowments such as clear air or fish stocks. Many other collective goods usually referred to as public goods are actually common goods. Public roads, for example, are non-rivalrous as long as there are few cars, but with enough traffic the road begins to get congested and each additional car lowers the value of the commons for others. At some point, congestion may become so bad that the road may cease to have any value at all. Although common goods are not public goods, institutions that protect them often are, thus making the challenge of establishing such institutions a social dilemma (Ostrom 1990).

So far we have assumed that benefits of the collective good increase monotonically with increasing levels of cooperation. Some goods, however, require that cooperation reach some threshold level before the good is provided. Voting is the most notable example of such a threshold or step good. As Figure 2.3 illustrates, up to the threshold level of cooperation, contributions to the good produce no marginal benefits. At the threshold, however, the calculus changes: it becomes beneficial to cooperate because the marginal benefit of cooperation is so large.

If, however, there are more than enough potential cooperators, there is a possibility of "overshooting" (which is the situation illustrated in the

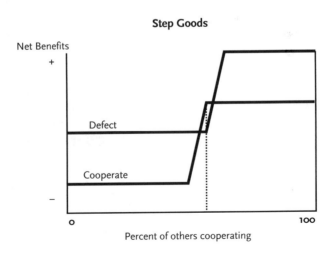

**Step Goods**

Net Benefits

Defect

Cooperate

0     100

Percent of others cooperating

Figure 2.3: Step Goods

figure), and the logic favoring cooperation quickly degenerates. Once above the threshold, defecting is again preferred to cooperating. From the perspective of the individual, the probability that one's contribution will be decisive depends on the likelihood that an efficacious group of precisely the right number will form, which in many circumstances is likely to be very low. (In an election, this would be the probability that your favored candidate won by exactly one vote.) When the size of the necessary group is large and the number of potential contributors is either unknown or is considerably larger than necessary, free riding, if not perfectly dominant, is nearly enough so that it remains a great temptation.

Interestingly, as Tuck (2008) has argued, if the number of potential cooperators is exactly the minimum needed to produce the good, every member of the group—not just the last cooperator—is responsible for the outcome. Collective action requiring consensus has this property. Under these circumstances, there is no free rider problem, since all can be thought of as the marginal contributor. This does not necessarily solve the collective action problem, however, since the situation is now essentially a stag hunt game, and the problem one of assurance, a structure that presents other challenges for collective action, as we will discuss below. Tuck argues further that the mere possibility of forming a coalition of precisely the right size eliminates the free rider problem. The problem with this line of thinking is that when there are more potential cooperators than necessary, many possible coalitions could supply the minimal group size. Without some institution to establish a group of just the right size and to assure each member that their contribution is pivotal, the complexity of strategic play will prevent any stable coalition from forming. There is, therefore, a second-order free rider problem in establishing such an institution, since the institution is a collective good for the larger community of potential cooperators.

Innumerable phenomena can be modeled as social dilemmas. Communities are better off if their members contribute to charities, join PTAs, refrain from littering, resist corruption, conserve water, observe the law without coercion, and otherwise choose to cooperate for the common good. In politics, nations are better off if their citizens inform themselves about political and policy issues, contribute to causes they care about, and turn out to vote. In international relations, the world would be better off if nations could cooperate to reduce climate change or eliminate nuclear weapons. In all of these circumstances we can see the free rider problem at work. The challenge, therefore, is to find a way to make cooperation the preferred strategy, to alter the calculus of cooperation.

## ASSURANCE

The problem of cooperation is not restricted to situations that can be modeled as a social dilemma. When the marginal benefits of cooperation depend on whether others also cooperate, the stag hunt game may be a better model. As Rousseau wrote, "If it was a matter of hunting a deer, everyone well realized that he must remain faithful to his post; but if a hare happened to pass within reach of one of them, we cannot doubt that he would have gone off in pursuit of it without a scruple" (Rousseau 1984, III). In a hunt in which the hunters encircle their prey, if all cooperate, the deer is caught. As long as each believes the others will stay at their post—that is, cooperate—cooperation is preferred to defection, since a share of the deer is preferred to the hare. If, however, there is reason to believe that others will leave their post, abandoning one's post becomes the more attractive choice, since the deer will likely escape. The problem, therefore, is one of mutual *assurance*—if all are assured that others will cooperate, each will too—which is why the stag hunt is also often referred to as an assurance game.

A two-party situation with essentially the same dynamic was suggested by David Hume. Two people are in a rowboat, each with one oar. If both row (cooperate), the boat goes forward. But if either one shirks (defects), there is no point in rowing, since the boat will go in circles (Hume, Nidditch, and Selby-Bigge 1978). Figure 2.4 models this situation as a two-party game. Note that there are two equilibria in this model, both cooperate and both defect. Neither is dominant, however, and the outcome depends on expectations. If A believes B will cooperate, then A should cooperate. If, however, A believes B will defect, A should defect.

The stag hunt described by Rousseau requires complete unanimity to keep the stag from escaping. A more general form of the problem, however, is depicted in Figure 2.5. When few others are cooperating, defection has a higher payoff. If a sufficient number of others cooperate, however, cooperation becomes the preferred strategy.

As with the two-party stag hunt, there are two equilibria in this game: *all cooperate* and *all defect*. For outcomes to the right of the point at which the individual payoffs to Cooperate equal those for Defect, any defector would wish to have cooperated. In relatively cooperative groups, therefore, there are pressures pushing for even greater cooperation. For outcomes to the left of the "tipping point" (Schelling 1960), however, any cooperator would wish to have defected. The implication, of course, is that individuals who expect low levels of cooperation by others will be tempted to defect. For this reason, expectations of the likely behavior of others—whether based

**An Assurance Game**

B

| | COOPERATE | DEFECT |
|---|---|---|
| **COOPERATE** | 3,3 | 1,2 |
| **DEFECT** | 2,1 | 2,2 |

A

Payoffs to 'A' listed first, to 'B' second. '3' is best and '1' is worst.

**Figure 2.4: Two-Party Assurance Game**
Party A chooses row, Party B chooses column. Party A's payoffs are given first, with 3 best and 1 worst.

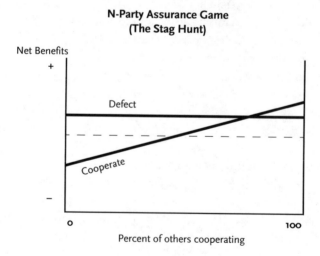

**N-Party Assurance Game
(The Stag Hunt)**

Net Benefits

Defect

Cooperate

Percent of others cooperating

**Figure 2.5:** Assurance Game (Stag Hunt)

on past experience, prevailing norms, credible commitments, or some other mechanism—tend to be self-reinforcing.

The problem of assurance can also be seen as a problem of commitment. If all could credibly commit to cooperate, the problem is solved. Indeed, once some critical number is committed to cooperation, others will find it in their interest to cooperate as well. The challenge for a player in a stag hunt, therefore, lies in knowing whether the commitment of others can be trusted, and, equally important, in demonstrating that her own commitment is trustworthy.

Compared to the social dilemma game, the cooperation problem posed by the stag hunt may seem less imposing, but that is not necessarily the case. The difficulty of reaching the cooperative equilibrium depends on expectations about the trustworthiness of others. If there is little reason to trust others, if a hare is worth nearly as much as (a share of) a deer, or if even small numbers of defectors can make defection the preferred strategy, then cooperation may be very difficult to achieve.

Many social interactions can be modeled as a stag hunt. To start with a simple example, the value of attending a party depends on what others decide to do. If a sufficient number of others show up, it would be desirable to be there too. But if others do not attend, it would be better to stay home. Bank runs can have the same structure. If others keep their money in the bank, it is best to keep to keep one's money there as well, but it may only take a rumor that others are pulling out to tip the system from cooperation to non-cooperation. A third class of collective goods, the *club good*, often presents a problem of assurance. Club goods are non-rivalrous but excludable. Examples are private clubs (of course) and cable television, situations in which the benefits of cooperating (i.e., joining) can be restricted to members. If the value of membership depends on how many others join as well, provision of the club good presents an assurance problem.

The significance of assurance for collective action is much greater than has been generally recognized, as Brian Skyrms (2004) has convincingly argued. In many situations, we will do our part, tell the truth, follow the rules, and be trustworthy *if* we are confident that others are also sharing the load, being honest, observing the rules, and acting in good faith. Norms of appropriate behavior and reciprocity, willingness to observe the law without coercion, and many other valuable social institutions depend on our belief that others, too, are observing them. Indeed, Rousseau's concept of the social contract depends on his construction of the fundamental problem facing society as a stag hunt. Whereas for Hobbes, voluntary cooperation was forever in peril and was, therefore, only possible through coercion, for Rousseau the social contract, once established, was self-enforcing. As

Skyrms (2004, 9) has noted, "[f]or a social contract theory to make sense, the state of nature must be an equilibrium. Otherwise there would not be the problem of transcending it. And the state where the social contract has been adopted must also be an equilibrium. Otherwise, the social contract would not be viable." The dividing line between Hobbes and Rousseau, therefore, can be seen as a dispute over whether society's fundamental problem is essentially a social dilemma or essentially a stag hunt.

When the collective action problem has the characteristics of a stag hunt, a variety of mechanisms can provide assurance and enable commitment. Institutions are particularly important, as I will explore in the next chapter. But, as I will argue in Chapter 7, narrative also can play a very important role in assurance, enabling us both to commit ourselves and to make those commitments credible to others.

## COORDINATING COOPERATION

Although a desire to cooperate in pursuit of collective goods is necessary, it may not be sufficient for collective action. Outside of simple games, in the real world of markets, politics, and social life, there are almost always many ways to achieve a collective goal. Television makers, program developers, and broadcasters would all benefit from the switch to high definition television, but what high-definition standard should prevail? Anti-war activists are outraged at US policy in Iraq, but how, where, and when should they gather to protest? Citizens want to help victims of a hurricane or a tsunami, but how should they channel their charitable giving? In these and many other circumstances, the problem is not only to overcome the temptation to free ride, but also to *coordinate* collective action.

Far from making cooperation easier, having more than one possibility for cooperation complicates matters. To take a very simple example, if two friends want to meet for dinner and there is only one restaurant in town, they will arrive at the same place without fail. But if there are many dining options, they will need to coordinate on where to meet. This problem is modeled in Figure 2.6 as a simple two-party coordination game in which A and B can cooperate in one of two ways, by choosing (I,I) or (II,II). Both cooperative solutions are equilibria. As depicted in the figure, the parties are indifferent between them.

The problem is to coordinate on one or the other of the solutions. This may seem trivial in the two-party, binary choice example, but when there are many parties and many options, coordination becomes increasingly difficult. To complicate matters, most situations have cooperative solutions

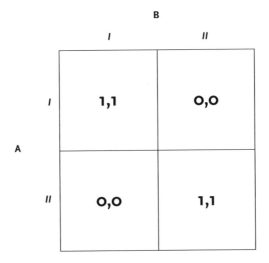

**A Coordination Game**

**B**

|  | *I* | *II* |
|---|---|---|
| *I* | 1,1 | 0,0 |
| *II* | 0,0 | 1,1 |

**A**

**Figure 2.6: Coordination**
Party A chooses row, Party B chooses column. Party A's playoffs are given first, with 1 best and 0 worst.

with differential impacts so that certain outcomes are preferred by some and other outcomes are preferred by others. Coordinating collective action is far more difficult with heterogeneous interests than with homogenous. To continue with the restaurant example, if one friend prefers Italian food and the other Indian, meeting either place may be better than not meeting at all, but there is a conflict of interest between the two of them.

This situation can be modeled as "battle of the sexes," so named because in the original formulation men and women are presumed to have different preferences with respect to possible cooperative outcomes (Luce and Raiffa 1957). As modeled in Figure 2.7, the game is only subtly different from the coordination game. There are two cooperative equilibria, (I,I) and (II,II), but A prefers the former and B the latter. Now the game may not be quite so easy to solve, since there is a competitive as well as a cooperative element to the situation. Of course, if one party can credibly commit to its preferred option, leaving a phone message that she will be at the Italian restaurant and then turning off her cell phone, for example, the other party will, logically, choose Italian as well.

Battle of the sexes can be considered a highly stylized version of a bargaining game, the essence of which is that both better could be better off if they can agree, but each has an incentive to seek a more favorable agreement, as when a buyer wants a low price and a seller wants a high price.

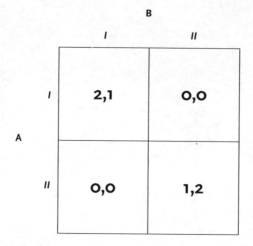

## Battle of the Sexes

Figure 2.7: Battle of the Sexes
Party A chooses row, Party B chooses column. Party A's playoffs are given first, with 2 best and 0 worst.

In principle, A and B should be able to solve their problem by negotiation. However, as the negotiation literature has amply demonstrated, overly aggressive "claiming" tactics (in which both parties commit to their favorite restaurant, for example, and each dines alone), poor communication about underlying interests, high levels of distrust, and sheer complexity can cause negotiations to fail even when agreement would yield substantial joint gains (Raiffa 1982).

As most collective goods admit a myriad of possible cooperative solutions, and as those solutions usually have differential effects on the parties involved, the essential dynamic of battle of the sexes is often at work. Combating climate change, for example, may be a collective good for the international community, but China and the United States, to note two of the important parties in the game, obviously have quite different interests with respect to the many possible cooperative outcomes.

Choreographing complex collective action among many actors with heterogeneous preferences is a difficult challenge. Certainly, institutions often serve to coordinate behaviors. In the civil rights movement, for example, even if all wanted to participate in collective action, there remained the question of what form cooperation should take: when to act, where to meet, and how to behave. The leadership structures of the civil rights movement—organizations such as the Southern Christian Leadership Council (SCLC) and the Student Non-violent Coordinating Committee (SNCC)—enabled organizers to formulate and distribute plans for protests that were credible to those who wished to participate. But, often choreography requires more than convening; it requires a shared vision of what collective action should look like, of the parts that each should be playing, and for that, I will argue in Chapter 7, the scripts of shared narratives can be enormously important.

## CONSTRUCTING COLLECTIVE GOODS

So far, our discussion of the problem of collective action has assumed that individuals share well-defined and stable interests in a collective good. Prisoners clearly want to avoid serving time, stag hunters want the deer, and friends want to meet for dinner. But treating interests as unproblematic misses a very important obstacle to collective action: the need to construct the common interest. Before we can gather to protest injustice, before we can combat climate change, before we can turn out to vote for our candidate, before we can engage in collective action in pursuit of any such ends, we need to have a common interest in them, and that is far from inevitable.

That the good might need to be constructed is usually ignored in the collective action literature. Indeed, a common interest is generally implicit in the definition of the problem. Yet, for those who would move a community to act collectively, common interests cannot be assumed. The basis for all interests is a good deal more unsettled than we usually admit. First, even if we posit some stable set of core interests—in power, wealth, security, and the like—it may not be obvious how some outcome actually affects these interests, and, therefore, what our interests are with respect to that outcome. Second, we have many interests that cannot be reduced to such core (and egoistic) interests, among them altruistic, ideological, and patriotic interests, all of which must be constructed. And, third, if interests are constructed, there arises a further problem: how to align individual interests into a common interest in a collective good. For these reasons, a broader conception of the problem of collective action needs to include consideration of how groups come to have common beliefs about consequences and common valuations of them.

Consider the problem of discerning how some act will affect our interests. This might at first inspection be seen as a simple matter of information provision, of "removing the blinders," but it is actually a good deal more problematic. Complex interests, even if related to fundamental desires such as wealth, power, and security, require a way of mapping from outcomes to those core desires. For example, textile factory workers clearly have an interest in job security, but for them to have an interest in opposing a free trade agreement requires some belief about the likely impact of that agreement on their job security. Similarly, Americans have an interest in preventing acts of terrorism on American soil, but having an interest in invading Iraq in order to prevent terrorism requires a complex set of beliefs. In both circumstances, beliefs mediate between outcome and interests, beliefs that must come from somewhere and that may or may not even be correct. Given the complexity of the causal linkage between these policy outcomes and impacts on personal well-being—even experts cannot agree—the question is how those beliefs are constructed.

A related point is that interests often depend on the salience of a problem. Unless one is aware of an issue, there can be no interest in it. Take, for example, the fate of the dodo, the now-extinct flightless bird that once inhabited Mauritius. At the time it was hunted into extinction, few were even aware of its peril, or even of its existence. Were it possible today, however, saving the dodo would now be an interest for conservationists (that is, it would have *existence value*), but at the time those who might have cared likely were not aware of the problem, and for that reason they had no interest in preserving it. To the extent that common interests depend on common beliefs and awareness, it becomes important to consider how communities learn about issues that might affect them. It is no accident, therefore, that much of what leaders of collective action do is raise the salience of issues and "educate" followers about their interests.

Interests may also be constructed in an even more fundamental sense. Once we get beyond core needs for food, shelter, security, affection, and the like, human interests cannot be explained without an understanding of the cultural and psychological factors that establish them. As the Nobel Prize–winning economist Thomas Schelling once noted, "most of the things that affect my welfare happen in my mind" (Schelling 1984, 333). The demand for many private goods—diamond engagement rings, Armani suits, or tickets to the Duke–North Carolina basketball game—no doubt relate to fundamental human desires, but they cannot be reduced to them. Indeed, as I have argued elsewhere (Mayer 1998), the value of these things depends on their symbolic meaning—that is, as I will argue in subsequent chapters, on their role in narratives about love, success, and tribal warfare, respectively.

Interests in collective goods are perhaps even more often constructed that those in private goods. Interests in fighting climate change or saving polar bears endangered by melting polar ice, in protecting rights to free speech or gun ownership, in ending the death penalty or abortion, in fighting child poverty or malaria in Africa, or in serving one's country or one's tribe, to take just a few examples, are far from given. None of these concerns can be reduced to their impact on private egoistic interests. Some are *altruistic* interests, based on concern for the fate of others. Some are *ideological* interests, based on a desire for one state of the world over another. Still others are *patriotic* interests, based on love of country or community. All are clearly constructed. And it is worth noting here an observation to which I will return in Chapter 6. Often it is the case that even when there are egoistic interests involved, for example, in opposing trade agreements to protect one's job or supporting war in Iraq to protect oneself, they are often re-constructed in non-egoistic terms when collective action is needed, as a matter of solidarity in the battle against corporate greed or as a matter of protecting America from her enemies.

The establishment of shared interests, even when it "merely" involves education about impacts on egoistic concerns and certainly when it involves non-egoistic altruistic, ideological, or patriotic motivations, is a matter that is often ignored by theories of collective action. But in practice, such construction is often a first and profound obstacle to collective action. Although there are other processes through which a community can come to hold common beliefs and interests, processes I will discuss in the next chapter, narratives play a particularly important role in constructing interests, and shared narratives in constructing common interests in collective goods.

# CHAPTER 3

# Theories of Collective Action and the Opening for Narrative

*Politics is the study of ways of solving collective action problems.*
Michael Taylor (1990, 224)

*Leaving stories out of account,...would mean renouncing the best clues about why people act as they do.*
Lewis P. Hinchman and Sandra Hinchman (1997, xiv)

The obstacles to successful collective action are formidable, but they are not insurmountable. The structure of many social situations inhibits cooperation unless the free rider problem can be overcome and/or parties can be assured of the cooperation of others. The complexity of many circumstances means that coordination may be difficult even when cooperation is clearly preferred. And, by all means not least, before there can be collective action, there must be convergence on a common understanding of interests. Given the obstacles to collective action, therefore, the puzzle is how humans, at least some of the time, actually do construct common interests, cooperate to pursue them, assure each other of their commitments, and coordinate their behavior to act collectively.

In subsequent chapters I will make the case for narrative as the most important human device for collective action. To see the value of a narrative theory of collective action, though, we first need to consider the other ways that scholars have sought to explain how humans do, sometimes, succeed in solving the problem. Broadly speaking, explanations for collective action can be grouped into three camps: rational choice, institutionalism, and social constructivism. Taken together, these schools of thought go far toward explaining the collective action we observe. Yet, for all the insights of the extant literature, important puzzles remain, puzzles that constitute an opening for a narrative theory of collective action.

## RATIONAL CHOICE

Rational choice approaches seek to explain collective action without abandoning the assumption of individual rationality implicit in the definition of the problem. In this paradigm, individuals are modeled as if they maximized a utility function.[1] It follows then that individuals who participate in collective action must be acting as if they were pursuing some set of interests. The focus of rational choice scholars has been on the problem of collective action given interests in some public good, and primarily on the free rider problem, usually modeled as a social dilemma and to a lesser extent on the problems of coordination and assurance. Rational choice has been generally unconcerned with the genesis of interests.

Hobbes offered one solution to the cooperation problem, that of the Leviathan, a central power able to compel cooperation or to enforce commitments. Most contemporary scholarly interest has focused on explaining cooperation in the absence of coercion or the ability to commit, however, either by positing additional interests that make cooperation rational or by considering the implications of repeated interactions. Olson's work provides the starting point for one line of attack, that of positing that when collective action occurs, individuals must be acting on the basis of interests other than an interest in the collective good. For large groups, Olson maintained, *selective incentives* are necessary for collective action. Selective incentives are benefits provided to individuals who cooperate (or costs imposed on those that do not) that do not depend on achievement of the collective good (Olson 1965, 51). Olson maintained for example, that workers join unions not because of the collective good of higher wages but because they are induced by material benefits of union membership, such as cheaper insurance, or because they are coerced, by closed shop rules, for example. Such selective incentives alter individuals' payoffs so that they no longer face a social dilemma.

Although Olson's primary focus was on public goods based on shared egoistic interests, the logic of collective action also applies to collective goods based on shared non-egoistic interests. As he put it, "the achievement of any common goal or the satisfaction of any common interest means that a public or collective good has been provided for that group" (Olson 1965, 15). In this book, I focus on three categories of non-egoistic goods that are often the basis for collective action. *Altruistic* collective goods arise when members of a group share an interest in the welfare of others, for example, a desire to aid victims of natural disasters such as Hurricane Katrina or the Haiti earthquake.[2] *Ideological* collective goods relate to preferences for certain states of the world over others, and include such things as saving endangered species, appointing conservative judges to the Supreme Court, or protecting freedom of expression. *Patriotic* collective goods involve concerns for the fortunes of one's tribe or nation, as when teammates sacrifice for the success of the team or citizens volunteer to fight for their country. These non-egoistic goods are often passionately desired (indeed, they are generally more likely to stir emotion than egoistic interests), but even with strongly held views on social justice, deep concerns for the plight of others, or intense fervor for the nation, the logic of collective action would still seem to make free riding the rational choice to the extent that enjoyment of the good does not depend on having contributed to its achievement.

As with economic associations, therefore, a group with an ideological, altruistic, or patriotic agenda might also induce cooperation by providing selective benefits. Advocacy organizations such as the National Rifle Association, for example, provide benefits such as firearms training or insurance discounts for their members in addition to their primary ideological mission of blocking gun control legislation. A related possibility is that individuals may enjoy non-material "solidarity" benefits from membership, in the form of friendship, approval, and the like. As Terry Moe (1980, 117) put it, "As with economic selective incentives, people who respond to solidarity inducements are generally joining for reasons that have nothing to do with politics."

That selective incentives can solve cooperation problems is not in dispute. But there are at least three limitations to this line of thinking. First, because selective incentives must be provided by some existing institution, the question arises: How was the institution formed in the first instance, since its existence may also be a collective good and its formation, therefore, may have required prior collective action? Second, separating selective benefits (a private good) from collective goods may not be fully possible, since it seems implausible that one would receive the same satisfaction from material benefits obtained from an organization whose ideological ambitions one opposes as from a group whose ends one supports (Chong 1991). Third, we see collective action in many circumstances in which there is no selective incentive of the kind Olson had in mind. People do not march in protest, join a campaign, or donate to a cause simply because they expect to receive material benefits.

If selective incentives are unavailable or insufficient, therefore, individuals engaged in collective action must be receiving benefits from acting itself—from joining, belonging, contributing, and participating—apart from whatever benefit they may get from the collective good. There is considerable evidence that actors involved in collective action are indeed often motivated by such *expressive* or *identity* interests. As Hirschman put it, "the very act of going after the public happiness is often the *next best thing* to actually *having* that happiness" (1982, 85–6; italics in the original). Hardin argues that individual identification with a group (all too often at the expense of other groups) allows self-interest "to be matched with group interest," so that individuals have an incentive to act as part of the group (Hardin 1995, 5). As with selective incentives, the enjoyment of expressive or identity interests is likely contingent on underlying interests in ends. It is hard to argue that individuals would receive much satisfaction from marching for a cause to which they do not subscribe or from affiliating with a group with whom they disagree. In his analysis of collective action in the American civil rights movement, Chong concludes that "political activists, it appears, not only wish to achieve particular political objectives, such as a change in government policy, and to fulfill their obligations, but also to voice their convictions, affirm their efficacy, share in the excitement of a group effort, and take part in the larger currents of history" (Chong 1991, 74).

Moreover, expressive benefits may also be contingent on belief in the possibility of success. Chong argues that usually we do not want to feel that we are wasting our time or that our cause is hopeless: "There may be some visceral relief but little expressive value to shouting in the wilderness" (Chong 1991, 91). This may be a bit too strong. Many groups have long survived with little prospect of achieving their goals: the libertarian party and anti–death penalty groups are examples. Perhaps a better formulation is that enjoyment of expressive or identity benefits is less contingent on attainment of ends than on the participation of others, that is, on participating in *collective* action, in which case the game is a stag hunt and the problem one of assurance.

Solutions to the assurance problem have received a good deal less attention in the rational choice literature, perhaps because they inevitably involve issues of beliefs and expectations not easily handled by the rational choice paradigm. Likewise, although rational choice theories nicely define the potential for coordination problems in situations with multiple possible solutions, they cannot predict outcomes without stepping outside the model.

The move by rational choice theorists to expand the possible motivations of actors to include ideological, altruistic or patriotic interests in *ends* and, more importantly, expressive or identity interests in *acting*, makes it possible to interpret virtually all observed collective action as rational choice. But once we accept that humans have interests beyond such basics as material gain, personal security, and the like—as surely we do—we need a theory *of* interests as well as a theory about the consequences of interests. How do humans come to care about the fate of others, of ideas, or of our community? How can a group of individuals arrive at shared interests in such ends? And why is it that members of a community of shared interests get satisfaction from acting in pursuit of those ends?

## Repeated Games and the Evolution of Cooperation

An alternative rational choice approach to explaining collective action is to consider how cooperation might arise through repeated play. Most of this literature has focused on iterated two-party prisoner's dilemma games. In the one-period prisoner's dilemma, the dominant strategy is unambiguously to defect. But if players know they will play many times (and particularly if they do not know which will be the last round), it may be quite rational to cooperate in one round if there is some prospect of inducing others to cooperate in subsequent rounds.

Robert Axelrod's enormously influential *The Evolution of Cooperation* (1984) provided the basis for much of the literature in this vein. Axelrod observed that sometimes cooperation occurs in the mostly unlikely of circumstances. During the trench warfare of World War I, for example, informal truces between the opposing armies broke out despite strenuous efforts by commanders on both sides to get the troops to fight. Axelrod's explanation was that the two sides' decisions of whether to hold back or attack (cooperate or defect) were influenced by the "shadow of the future" (Axelrod 1984), the knowledge that whatever temporary advantage might be had by attacking would be lost through resumption of a battle that would leave both sides worse off.

This intuition was developed further in a computer tournament pitting different strategies against each other in repeated two-party prisoner's dilemma games. The strategy of "Always Defect" can never lose to another strategy. But against most strategies, it will also fail to elicit cooperation, with the consequence that both parties end up in a "Defect, Defect" cycle. The winning strategy in the tournament was "Tit for Tat," a relatively "nice" strategy, which begins by cooperating, only defects if its partner defects, and resumes cooperating as soon as its partner does too. "Tit for Tat" won not because it beat its partners (indeed it can *never* do so), but because it was most effective in eliciting cooperation from others.

The shadow of the future can be thought of as transforming repeated prisoner's dilemma games into a one-period stag hunt (Skyrms 2004). If, for example, the strategic choice is framed as a binary choice between a cooperative strategy such as "Tit for Tat" or a non-cooperative strategy such as "Always Defect," the game is a stag hunt, since "Tit for Tat" is optimal if others also play it. This is a profound observation of great significance for thinking about how institutions become established in society. Members of a community interacting with each other over time may be able to solve their social dilemma through conventions such as reciprocity that are quite stable once established.

The appeal of the repeated games metaphor is that it provides a logic in which cooperation that might not be rational in one-period games becomes consistent with rationality, and does so without recourse to positing additional interests. The appeal is reinforced by the observation that groups in which there are high levels of cooperation have an advantage over groups that do not, suggesting an evolutionary pressure towards cooperation. And, as we will explore shortly, these logics provide a solid rational choice basis for the genesis of all manner of institutions.

We should not be too quick to assume that the iterated games framework is sufficient to explain collective action, however. First, if there is an end point to the game and parties know when the final round will occur, rational behavior will not lead to cooperation. Knowing that the dominant strategy in the final round is defection, defection becomes dominant in the penultimate round (since there is no possibility of inducing future cooperation), and so forth.

Second, cooperation, even if achieved, may be unstable. In social dilemmas involving many parties, non-cooperators may be able to exploit the gullibility of cooperators in the absence of mechanisms for sanctioning or excluding them. Even in stag hunt games, where we tend to assume that cooperative institutions will be stable once arrived at, the presence of "hare hunters" in a community can unravel cooperation (Skyrms 2004).

Third, in order that there be repeated play, some institution must structure the interaction. The question then arises: What structures the structure? Some rules, it seems, must be exogenous to the rational choice model.

Fourth, with respect to the problem of cooperation in pursuit of public goods, repeated play cannot explain how cooperation occurs when there is little shadow of the future. We see cooperation in many circumstances in which collective action involves large numbers of actors—engaged in voting, contributing to causes, marching in protest, for example—who are not involved in repeated play, indeed whose choices will likely not even be observed by others with whom they "play." A truce in the interminable stalemate of WWI trench warfare is one thing (and even then one suspects there was more to the story than iteration), the extraordinary level of spontaneous cooperation among rescuers in the immediate aftermath of the 9/11 attacks is quite another.

For all of these reasons, the model in which cooperation, assurance, and coordination arises out of repeated play among hyper-rational individuals clearly needs to be supplemented, at minimum, by other models that provide a richer account of the institutional context in which games are played and a more nuanced depiction of human behavior.

## INSTITUTIONALISM

A second broad approach to explaining collective action credits institutions—formal rules, laws, contracts, treaties, and the like, as well as informal norms and social conventions—with facilitating collective action. Institutions can enable cooperation in social dilemmas, assurance in stag hunts, or coordination when there is more than one cooperative solution.

Historically, institutionalism was largely blind to the problem of collective action. In sociology, structural-functionalists in the tradition of Émile Durkheim and Talcott Parsons assumed that institutions simply arose to serve a needed function in society. In political science, the pluralist school in American politics (Bentley 1949; Truman 1951; Dahl 1961) made much the same assumption. Olson's sharp formulation of the problem of collective action skewered the complacency of functionalist theories of collective action, however, with the result that institutionalism was on the defensive for many years.

More recently, a renewed interest in institutions as solutions to collective action problems has emerged in conjunction with the burgeoning "new institutionalist" literature (Williamson 1975; North 1990; Ostrom 1990). This literature can be classified in many ways (Hall and Taylor 1996). For our purposes, however, it is most useful to distinguish between *rational* and *behavioral* institutionalism, which differ with regard to their underlying psychological assumptions, and, therefore, to both the genesis and the function of social institutions.

### Rational Institutionalism

Rational institutionalism shares with rational choice the presumption that individuals can be treated as in they were interest maximizers. The goal of this literature is to demonstrate "[h]ow rationality on the part of individuals leads to coherence at the level of society," as Robert Bates (1988, 399) has put it. But to a much greater extent than rational choice theory, rational institutionalism emphasizes that individuals are embedded in institutions that constrain choice, alter incentives, and limit information, and, therefore, calls attention to the form of those institutions. For rational institutionalists, institutions help solve collective action problems by conferring selective benefits (Olson) and reducing costs of cooperating (Tarrow 1994). They promote cooperative agreements by facilitating negotiation processes (Raiffa 1982; Elster 1989), enabling commitment (North 1990), and enforcing contracts (Williamson 1975). They provide assurance (Skyrms 2004). And they transform one-time encounters into repeated games (Axelrod 1984). Institutions may be particularly important for coordinating collective action. Conventions allow parties to anticipate the choices of others and thereby effectively limit the domain of possible solutions. Driving on the right, a common Internet protocol, the meaning of words, and many other social conventions are essentially solutions to coordination problems.

Rational institutionalists generally treat institutions as the artifact of repeated games among rational actors. In this regard, the approach is fully compatible with one strand of rational choice theory. But, and this is the key point of departure, once established, institutions are "sticky." In any given interaction, therefore, some institutions will be exogenous. As Ostrom puts it, "all rules are nested in another set of rules that determine how the first set of rules can be changed" (Ostrom 1990, 51). It is useful to note that once institutions are established, the question of whether or not to adhere to them has many of the properties of a stag hunt. As long as others observe the rules, it may be better to do so as well, particularly if defection seems likely to lead to the dissolution of valuable social structures. The persistence of institutions established in prior periods makes outcomes path-dependent (Keohane 1984; Bates 1988).

Rational institutionalism has provided a powerful explanatory framework for many forms of collective action, including institutions for governing environmental commons (Hardin 1982, Ostrom 1990; Young 1994), opportunity structures in social movements (Tarrow 1994), regimes in international relations (Krasner 1983; Keohane 1984), and voluntary associations in civic life (Putnam 1993). Strict adherence to rational choice assumptions poses several problems for institutional theory, however, as many of these scholars have noted, including Ostrom (1998) and Putnam (1993).

First, institutions can only arise through this mechanism when there are well-structured interactions with multiple iterations and no clear endpoint, the same critique made above of the repeated games literature. Ostrom (1990) documents how members of small communities engaged in repeated interactions can construct local common pool resource institutions. In these circumstances, the shadow of the future is long, the benefits of establishing rules clear, and the costs of violating manifest. But not every situation in which we observe successful collective action has these characteristics.

Second, if rules are established in a game played according to a prior set of rules, the obvious question is where the prior rules came from. One could argue that the structuring institutions were themselves the outcomes of even earlier games, and the institutions that structured those games of yet even earlier encounters, and so on, but such infinite regress is ultimately unsatisfactory.[3] Ostrom (1990) deals with the problem by positing a hierarchy of institutions, in which some rules are more fundamental and less easily changed than others, and which can, therefore, be treated as exogenous, but that approach requires stepping outside of the rational institutionalist model.

Third, and most compelling, the behavioral assumptions underlying rational institutionalism are often simply unrealistic. Rational choice requires that individuals behave as if they could identify options, predict consequences, and value outcomes in terms of a stable, accessible, and consistent set of interests. That humans can behave in this manner is not in doubt. In economic decision-making, for example, when individuals repeatedly face the same choice circumstance (North 1990, 19), or when the stakes are high enough, the assumption of individual rationality may be quite reasonable. Schumpeter, for example, argued that "[t]he assumption that conduct is prompt and rational is in all cases a fiction. But it proves to be sufficiently near to reality, if things have had time to hammer logic into men" (quoted in Winter 1986, 248).[4] Yet, the evidence is overwhelming that the assumption of rationality is often simply wrong. We perceive selectively and often wrongly, fail to remember most things than happen and "remember" some that don't, engage in limited searches for options, rely extensively on heuristics and other mental shortcuts rather than process information analytically, fail to anticipate the impact of our actions on our interests, "satisfice" rather than maximize, and otherwise behave in ways that violate basic tenets of rational choice.

### Institutional Behaviorism

In contrast to rational institutionalism, *institutional behaviorism* assumes, at most, "bounded rationality" (Simon 1969). Humans avoid "cognitive dissonance" (Festinger 1957). They are "cognitive misers" (Taylor 1981) who cling to familiar patterns of thought. In the last 30 years, an explosion of work in the cognitive sciences—in psychology, behavioral economics, neurobiology and related fields—convincingly demonstrates the biological limits to our analytic capacity. Although there is great variation in the literature, a common tenet is that these limits force humans to rely on an institutionalized environment that structures our thinking and behavior. As Herbert Simon put it, "[h]uman beings, viewed as behaving systems, are quite simple. The apparent complexity of our behavior over time is largely a function of the complexity of the environment in which we find ourselves" (1969, 53).

Research in the cognitive sciences has spawned a large and growing behavioral economics literature that seeks to incorporate a more realistic view of human nature into economic thought. Daniel Kahneman and Amos Tversky have been the most influential figures in the field (Kahneman and Tversky 1979; Kahneman, Slovic, and Tversky 1982). In a series of experiments, they demonstrated that individual preferences under uncertainty could be manipulated by framing logically identical situations as avoidance of loss or opportunity for gain. Their subsequent work identified a number of other predictable anomalies, among them anchoring on irrelevant information, availability biases, and overweighting of low probabilities (Tversky and Kahneman 1990; Kahneman 2011). These and other similar concepts have been applied to consumer choice (Thaler 1980; Thaler and Shefrin 1981), financial markets (Shleifer 2000), and a wide range of other topics (Ariely 2008; Akerlof and Shiller 2009; Thaler and Sunstein 2009).

The psychological assumptions underlying institutional behaviorism differ considerably from those of rational choice and rational institutionalism. First, to a very great extent, human thought is schematic rather than analytic. It is structured by pre-existing schemas, "data structures for representing the generic concepts stored in memory" (Rumelhart and Ortony 1977, 101). Schemas organize our world into categories, things sufficiently similar to constitute a type: a "car," a "tree," a "liberal," and so on (Lakoff 1987). Associated with these types are certain attributes. "Lumberjacks" are people who wear flannel shirts, live vigorously, and like their beer (Strauss and Quinn 1997, 48). Understanding, therefore, is essentially an act of recognition, of slotting the unfamiliar into familiar patterns.

Second, human behavior is more a matter of routine than of choice. If understanding is determined by schema, and understanding drives intentions, behavior will reflect our schematized environment. Some schemas affect behavior even more directly by scripting our routines such that behavior is more a matter of habit than of choice. When I drive home from work, I don't have to choose. I get in my car, turn on the radio and think about the news, and discover 10 minutes later that I'm home (which is fine unless I was supposed to pick up some milk on the way).

As Douglass North has argued, a theory of institutions based on bounded rationality is on stronger ground than one that insists on classical rationality (North 1990). First, behavioralist assumptions allow norms of reciprocity and fairness to operate even in situations where their application appears "irrational." In experiments with repeated prisoner's dilemma games with a finite number of rounds, for example, players appear to use heuristics of reciprocity rather than backward induction logics and therefore cooperate more than rational choice would predict (Camerer and Fehr 2006). Similarly, experiments with ultimatum and dictator games consistently find that players do not choose the "optimal" strategy of making extreme offers but rather behave in ways that reflect norms of fairness.[5]

Ernst Fehr and Urs Fischbacher (2005) describe strong reciprocity as a form of social preference in which payoffs to an individual depend on the perceived appropriateness of others' behavior: "A strongly reciprocal individual responds kindly toward actions that are perceived to be kind and hostilely toward actions that are perceived to be hostile. Whether an action is perceived to be kind or hostile depends on the fairness or unfairness of the intension underlying the action" (Fehr and Fischbacher 2005, 153). The idea of strong reciprocity is similar to Margaret Levi's (1997) concept of contingent consent. Levi finds that in situations in which free riding would predict little citizen consent, "consent is contingent on the perceived fairness of both government and other citizens" (Levi 1997, 3).

Strong reciprocity transforms the payoffs in social dilemmas, making it desirable to cooperate if others do and to defect if they don't (Fehr, Fischbacher, and Gachter 2002). In this sense, then, the reciprocity norm is a device for converting repeated prisoner's dilemmas into stag hunts. Moreover, belief that others are reciprocators allows parties to know that cooperation will be met with cooperation, thus solving the assurance problem. In Putnam's terms, a society with high levels of such beliefs could be said to have a high level of social capital and, therefore, be expected to have higher levels of cooperation more generally (Putnam 1993), And under some circumstances, the reciprocity norm may be strong enough that third parties step in to punish unfair behavior, as Fehr, Fischbacher and Gachter (2002) have found. The social norm of strong reciprocity, therefore, is an enforcement mechanism for other social norms.

Evolutionary game theorists have found that relaxing assumptions about rationality allows for better explanations of the role of history in the genesis and stability of new institutions. Expectations of likely future actions are based on perceptions of past actions. Oran Young, for example, argues that

> agents are not perfectly rational and fully informed about the world in which they live. They base their decisions on fragmentary information, they have incomplete models of the process they are engaged in, and they may not be especially forward looking. Still, they are not completely irrational. They adjust their behavior based on what they think other agents are going to do, and these expectations are generated endogenously by information about what other agents have done in the past (Young 1998, 8)

Similarly, Bo Rothstein (2000) emphasizes the importance of perceived group history in enabling trust to evolve. Rothstein argues that the collective memory of the group is "the missing link in the theory of social capital and game-theoretical explanations of cooperation" (Rothstein 2000, 477). A common interpretation of the past solves the problem of predicting behavior for large groups in which there are not likely to be repeated interactions among all individuals. We will take up the nature and bases of collective memory in Chapter 6.

Behaviorist assumptions also make clearer how institutions help coordinate collective action when there are many forms cooperation could take, particularly when cooperative outcomes have differential effects on interested parties (as in the "battle of the sexes" game). To the extent that parties engage in limited search for solutions and are willing to "satisfice" (Simon 1969) rather than "maximize," precedents, conventions, and shared norms are all the more effective as coordinating mechanisms (Allison 1971; Steinbruner 1974). In a world of limited search, conventions, once established, become routines. And focal points, prominent features of the environment, facilitate coordination in large part because they automatically suggest themselves. Bounded rationality thus provides further perspective on institutional stability and, therefore, on path dependency, since institutions do not have to be optimal to persist.

Finally, behavioral theory begins to point the way towards an understanding of how communities might converge on a common understanding of their interests, a question on which rational choice and rational institutionalist theories are silent. To the extent that interests almost always embody an element of belief about the world, and that understandings are schematic, it follows that shared schemas can help create common interests. Confronted with an apparent act of aggression by a foreign leader, for example, a schema of the form "bullies cannot be appeased" would lead to a shared "interest" in using force in response.

Institutional behaviorism goes far in advancing our understanding of collective action. But there are limits to this approach as well. First, the paradigm is most persuasive in routine circumstances. When parties interact repeatedly, common schemas can emerge, trust and reciprocity norms operate, and conventions evolve to enable collective action. Institutional behavior is less satisfactory for explaining collective action in unique circumstances, however. Of course institutions mattered for the 1963 March on Washington at which King gave his "I Have a Dream" speech: the civil rights movement was highly organized, the press had experience covering protests, and the public had schemas for interpreting what they heard on the news. But a gathering of 100,000 for a one-time event cannot be reduced to routine behavior.

Second, behavioral theories cannot fully account for either the genesis or the transmission of social schemas. Schema theory generally sees schemas as the residue of experience. Sandra Marshall, for example, asserts that "[s]chemas develop after many similar and repeated experiences, each of which constitutes a problem for the individual" (Marshall 1995). This may be true for some schemas, such as my driving routine to work, but it cannot be true for all. I am not a lumberjack and have never met one, but I have a schema for lumberjacks. Clearly, the vast majority of schemas in mind must be imported from culture. Those cultural schemas might merely be the distillation of a group's past experiences. One can see how a community might converge on stereotypes of used car salesmen, for example, which could then be conveyed in some fashion even to first-time car buyers. But clearly not all cultural schemas arise out of actual experience. To take an extreme example, consider the persistence of racist stereotypes: about the corruption of Jews in Nazi Germany, or the bestiality of blacks in the Jim Crow South, or the savagery of "Indians" in colonial America, or even, in 19th-century Boston, the intellectual inferiority of the Irish. It is hard to argue that such schemas are the product of experience, since they are false. Clearly, some schema must be generated and transmitted through other mechanisms.

But the greatest limitation of an institutional behaviorist approach to collective action is that it provides an incomplete account of motive. That much of our thought is schematic is clear, that many of our behaviors are habit is evident, but taken to the extreme this line of thought grants so much explanatory power to institutions that it comes close to denying agency. And there is something bloodless about this characterization of behavior. Missing is an explanation for why we care so passionately about our causes, for how it might be that we derive satisfaction from expression itself. As North conceded about the limitations of institutional approaches, "We simply do not have any convincing theory of the sociology of knowledge that accounts for the effectiveness (or ineffectiveness) of organized ideologies or accounts for choices made when the payoffs to honesty, integrity, working hard, or voting are negative" (North 1990, 42).

## SOCIAL CONSTRUCTIVISM

A third way of thinking about the nature of social behavior, and, therefore, potentially of explaining collective action, is social constructivism. Like the rational choice and institutional schools, social constructivism is a big camp. At its core, however, are two propositions: first, that shared symbols, ideas, ideologies, narratives, religions, and other ideational structures of culture are essential to understanding human behavior; and, second, that these structures arise out of and propagate through processes of social discourse and communication.

Constructivist thinking has its intellectual roots in the work of George Herbert Mead (1934), Frederic Bartlett (1932), Lev Vygotsky (1978, 1986), Kenneth Burke (1945), and Claude Lévi-Strauss (1966), all of whom explored the extent to which, as Burke put it, man is "[s]eparated from his natural condition by instruments of his own making" (Burke and Gusfield 1989, 67). Constructivist scholarship has been enormously influential in many fields. In cultural anthropology the writings of Victor Turner (1974) and Clifford Geertz (1973) revitalized interest in symbolism. In cultural studies, Michel Foucault (1972), and Jacques Derrida (1976) focused attention on the role of language and other signs as instruments of power. Peter Berger and Thomas Luckman's *The Social Construction of Reality* (1966) had a tremendous impact across the social sciences. Jerome Bruner (1986, 1990), James Wertsch (1985, 1991, 1998), and many others were influential in the study of social foundations of education.

Constructivism has made fewer inroads in political science, with some notable exceptions. In political communication, Murray Edelman's "symbolic politics" (1964) and Erving Goffmann's concept of "frames"—defined as "schemata of interpretation" that enable individuals "to locate, perceive, identify, and label" occurrences in the world (Goffman 1974, 21)—were taken up by a number of scholars, among them George Lakoff (Lakoff and Johnson 1980; Lakoff 1987), Lance Bennett (Bennett 1983), Doris Graber (Graber 1984), Deborah Stone (Stone 1988), William Gamson (Gamson 1992), and Robert Entman (Entman 1993; Entman 2003). And in international relations, John Ruggie (1982, 1998), Benedict Anderson (1983), Alexander Wendt (1992, 1999), Peter Katzenstein (1996), Margaret Keck and Kathryn Sikkink (1998), and Martha Finnemore (1998) spawned a now considerable body of work exploring the role of ideas in shaping the international order.

Social constructivism differs from both rational choice and institutional behaviorism with regard to its psychological assumptions. In the social constructivist paradigm, human behavior is fundamentally a form of symbolic expression, enabled by our psychological predilection for symbolic thinking and our immersion in a symbolic culture of signs, ideologies, rituals, myths, and other such constructs. As Vygotsky put it, "[t]he use of signs leads humans to a specific structure of behavior that breaks away from biological development and creates new forms of a culturally-based psychological process" (Vygotsky 1978). From this it follows that "[m]ental processes can be understood only if we understand the tools and signs that mediate them" (Wertsch 1985, 15). Language is particularly important. It is at once "the central vehicle through which we negotiate agreements about the real and the good," and "a form of prison" that limits our thought (Wertsch 1985, 37). So, too, are the tropes of culture, including shared narratives.

The constructivist perspective has a number of significant implications. First, human experience of reality (to the extent that it admits of such a thing) is heavily mediated by symbolic constructions. As Burke eloquently states,

> The symbol using animal, yes, obviously. But can we bring ourselves to realize just what that formula implies, just how overwhelmingly much of what we mean by *reality* has been built up for us through nothing but our symbol systems? . . . . [H]owever important to us is the tiny sliver of reality each of us has experienced firsthand, the overall "picture" is but a construct of our symbol systems . . . (Burke and Gusfield 1989).

It follows, therefore, that how we understand the world is not determined by external reality, but rather reflects "the social construction of reality" (Berger and Luckmann 1966).

Second, human understanding is less a matter of either analytical reasoning or routinized schemas than it is of analogical processes. We don't simply slot experience into familiar schema, we take metaphoric leaps to establish meaningful patterns. As Lakoff and Mark Johnson put it, metaphors provide "the only ways to perceive and experience much of the world" (Lakoff and Johnson 1980). Moreover, memory itself is not a stable record of what actually happened, but is, rather, a reconstruction in service of our meaning making. As Bartlett wrote, "remembering appears to be far more decisively an affair of construction rather than one of mere reproduction" (Bartlett 1932, 205). And because memory is a meaning making activity, and meaning arises from social construction, the form of our memory is also at least partly socially constructed, which makes it possible to speak of collective memory (Halbwachs and Coser 1992).

Third, emotion not only colors cognition, it also enables it in important ways. The relationship between feeling and thinking turns out to be far more complex than we once imagined, as Forgas (2008) and others have explored. Certainly our affective states influence our perceptions, sometimes in distorting ways, by compelling us to construct understandings that are consistent with our emotional stances. But affect is also functional in calling our attention to that which is important, in orienting ourselves towards potential dangers or opportunities, and in enabling memory, on which, of course, we depend for cognition. As Bartlett noted about his memory experiments, "When a subject is being asked to remember, very often the first thing that emerges is something of the nature of an attitude. The recall is then a construction, made largely on the basis of this attitude, and its general effect is that of a justification of the attitude" (Bartlett 1932, 205).

Finally, constructivist theories tend to differ from both rational choice and behaviorist models with respect to motive. For constructivists, humans are stirred by passions as much as by reason or habit, driven by a need to imbue experience with meaning, and motivated by a desire to establish identity. Constructivist theory, therefore, gives a much better account of why humans might care passionately about the plight of others, the advancement of a cause, or the fate of the nation, interests that rational choice theory might acknowledge but cannot explain.

Although constructivist approaches have been widely adopted in some social science fields, and more recently have begun to be taken up in some subfields of political science, few constructivists have focused directly on the problem of collective action, perhaps because strong constructivist assumptions come close to denying that there is a collective action problem. At the extreme, social construction drives individual agency out of the equation, so much credit is given to the constructions themselves. And if culture were determinative, the problems of free riding, assurance and coordination would largely disappear. A more promising line of thought, on which I will draw in Chapter 6, takes the view that we "live in the middle" (Wertsch 1998), that we are both shaped by and shapers of our culture. As Clifford Geertz put it, humans are "[a]n animal suspended in webs of significance he himself has spun..." (Geertz 1973, 5).

One notable exception to the indifference to collective action among constructivists is the "new social movement" literature, an explicitly constructivist approach to the problem (Snow, Benford, Rochford, and Worden 1986; Snow and Benford 1988; Gamson 1992; Keck and Sikkink 1998; Benford 2000; McAdam, Tarrow, Sidney, and Tilly 2001; Tilly 2002; Tilly 2004). This literature builds on one strand of constructivist thought, that of Goffman's (1974) concept of frames. A frame serves to answer the question "What is it that is going on here?" Goffman's point was that for any event there are always multiple possible interpretations, which opens the door for communication to affect the answer.

The concept of framing is often left a bit undefined in the literature, but perhaps Entman's is the clearest formulation: "To frame is to select some aspects of a perceived reality and make them more salient in a communicating text, in such a way as to promote a particular problem definition, causal interpretation, moral evaluation, and/or treatment recommendation of the item described" (Entman 1993, 51). It is important to recognize that the impact of frames depends crucially on how they resonate with schemas categories, scripts, or stereotypes that already exist in the mind (Entman 1993, 53).

In applying framing theory to collective action, Robert Benford and David Snow argue that collective action is enabled by "collective action frames" that operate by "assigning meaning to and interpreting relevant events and conditions in ways that are intended to mobilize potential adherents and constituents, to garner bystander support, and to demobilize antagonists" (Snow and Benford 1988, 198). Similarly, Margaret Keck and Kathryn Sikkink define collective action frames as "conscious strategic efforts by groups of people to fashion shared understandings of the world and of themselves that legitimate and motivate collective action" (Keck and Sikkink 1998, 3). A necessary condition for social movements is that participants share a common frame. Snow et al (1986, 464) suggest that communities converge on a common frame through a process of "frame alignment," defined as "the linkage of individual and SMO [social movement organization] interpretive orientations, such that some set of individual interests, values and beliefs and SMO activities, goals, and ideology are congruent and complementary."

For Benford and Snow (2000), frame adoption depends on "cultural resonance." A frame that fits the ideology and values of a community will be more likely adopted than one that does not. New frames are possible, but they must be based in the extant culture:

> The cultural material most relevant to movement framing processes include the extant stock of meanings, beliefs, ideologies, practice, values, myths, narratives,

and the like, all of which...constitute the cultural resource base from which new cultural elements are fashioned, such as innovative collective action frames, as well as the lens through which framings are interpreted and evaluated" (Benford and Snow 2000, 629).

Framing theory offers an alternative description of the motivation of actors in at least some collective action contexts, one that begins to explain how a community of individuals might arrive at a common interpretation of the collective good, might be sufficiently motivated to take up arms as an act of identity affirmation, and might converge on a coordinated strategy for such action. Where rational choice theory fails to explain the basis of shared beliefs about common interests in ends, or the source of expressive or identity benefits from participating in collective action in pursuit of those ends framing theory seems to fill the void. Where institutional accounts miss the passion and dynamism that so often accompanies collective action, framing theory offers a perspective on how groups might muster the passions needed to overcome the logic of collective action.

Framing theory, however, is much better at describing what happens in collective action than at explaining how frames are constructed and adopted, and, how, exactly, they motivate action. To define a collective action frame as a shared construct that motivates individuals to act collectively comes close to tautology. That such ideational constructs exist and that they are often crucial to collective action seems clear. But to demonstrate that frames matter is not to explain their genesis, their attraction, or their power.

Moreover, we need to explain how frames align individual and collective identity. As William Gamson observed, "participation in social movements frequently involves enlargement of personal identity for participation and offers fulfillment and realization of the self" (Gamson 1992, 56). For this reason, he argues, "[a]ny movement that hopes to sustain commitment over a period of time must make the construction of a collective identity one its most central tasks" (Gamson 1991, 27). But the question is how frames might actually do this. As Benford and Snow note, "the question of how participation precipitates the enlargement of personal identity, or the correspondence between individual and collective identities, has not been satisfactorily answered by scholars investigating this linkage" (2000, 631).

## THE OPENING FOR NARRATIVE

The extensive literatures that seek to explain collective action provide a rich array of insights. But, as we have explored in this chapter, each of the major paradigms has its limitations. Even taking them together, important puzzles remain, puzzles that create an opening for a narrative theory of collective action.

Rational choice theories based on narrowly egoistic interests have quite limited application in explaining collective action. Allowing a much expanded list of ideological, altruistic, or patriotic interests in ends, and expressive or identity interests in acting, greatly enlarges the domain of collective action to which the theory applies. But rational choice is silent on the basis of those interests. It cannot explain, therefore, *why* we might care about earthquake victims in Haiti or the impacts of climate change on future generations. Moreover, although it postulates expressive or identity interests, it has little to say about how they arise or why they move us. As George Akerlof and Rachel Kranton write in the conclusion to *Identity Economics*, which makes a persuasive case for considering norms and identity as fundamental motives in economic and social life, there remains a deep question: "Where do norms and identity come from? How do they evolve and change?" (Akerlof and Kranton 2010, 130).

The repeated games approach gets around the need to invoke expressive or identity interests by demonstrating the ways in which cooperation in pursuit of collective goods can evolve. Yet this mechanism, alone, would seem to apply to only a limited set of circumstances, those in which there is repeated play among the same actors with no known endpoint. Rational institutionalism, built upon the repeated games foundation, answers the last question largely by assuming that institutions that evolve in one period are "sticky" in the next. There remains, however, something of a problem of infinite regress, which is the question of what structures the structure.

Institutional behaviorism builds from psychological assumptions that are more consistent with empirical evidence and that provide a more solid grounding for institutional theory. We are in fact quite bounded in our rationality, we rely on broad schema to interpret experience, and we behave according to well-established habits and norms, but these limits may actually serve to facilitate cooperation, provide assurance about others' behaviors, and reinforce conventions that coordinate collective action. Generalized norms of reciprocity, social capital and other social institutions are particularly important in this regard. But behavioral theory provides an inadequate account of the genesis and transmission of particular beliefs, values, and interests, of the passion and affirmation of personal identity that so often accompanies collective action; and of the often dramatic and spontaneous in collective action.

Social constructivist approaches offer a way of accounting for a fuller array of human motivations and suggests a more creative and flexible mechanism for collective action. Framing theory is particularly useful for suggesting that symbolic constructions shape our apprehensions and trigger our emotions, and, therefore, for recognizing how a shared frame might lead to a common interpretation of interests. Shared frames, because they also suggest a program of action, may also help coordinate cooperation by providing a shared script. Clearly, frames matter. But missing is a theory that can more fully explain how frames are constructed, how they are transmitted and shared, and, most importantly, how they stir our passions, engage our identity, and move us towards collective action.

What remains is an opening for narrative, indeed a demand for it. Each of the theoretical frameworks—rational choice, institutionalism, and constructivism—provides considerable insight into the nature of the collective action problem and its solutions. But all leave questions unanswered. What is the basis for non-egoistic interests, and how are identity and expressive interests formed and invoked? If we rely on memory of the past to create rules of thumb or other schema, either individually or collectively, what structures that memory? If we are creatures of passion, what triggers our outrage at unfairness and our hunger for justice? And, how can a group of individuals come to a common understanding of their interests, a shared consciousness of their circumstance, and a united passion for collective action?

In the chapters that follow, I argue for a narrative theory of collective action. My claim is that narrative is perhaps *the* essential human tool for collective action, a tool of enormous power and flexibility for constructing shared purposes, making participation in collective action an affirmation of personal identity, providing assurance that others will join us in the cause, and choreographing coordinated acts of meaning. Before we can fully appreciate the role of narrative in collective action, however, first we need to consider more carefully the role of narrative in the individual mind and the persuasive power of story, to which I turn in the next section of this book.

PART TWO

*Narrative, Mind, and Motive*

## CHAPTER 4

# The Storytelling Animal

*Now a whole is that which has a beginning, middle, and end.*
(Aristotle 1947, 634)

*The natural flights of the human mind are not from pleasure to pleasure, but from hope to hope.*
Samuel Johnson (1785, 6)

Whatever else we are, we humans are a storytelling animal. As Barbara Hardy has said, we "dream in narrative, daydream in narrative, remember, anticipate, hope, despair, believe, doubt, plan, revise, criticize, construct, gossip, learn, hate and live by narrative" (Hardy 1968, 5). So ubiquitous is narrative, though—in our play, our work, and our politics— that it is hard to recognize the full extent and implications of our narrativity. In this chapter, therefore, I explore the psychological implications of our immersion in narrative. I will argue that stories play important roles in cognition, emotion, identity, and, ultimately, action. To understand how narrative serves these functions, however, it is necessary first to have a clear understanding of what a story is. I begin, therefore, with a discussion of the key elements of narrative.

### THE NARRATIVE CODE

What is a story? Few things are more familiar, but perhaps because narrative is so familiar, the concept is surprisingly hard to pin down when we seek to define it. We know a story when we hear one, but defining what is and is not a story is not so simple. No clear consensus exists in the scholarly literature. Structuralists tend to focus on form, defining story largely in terms of plot: "Narrative...may be defined as the representation of real or fictive events and situations in a time sequence" (Prince 1982, 1). Moreover, the sequences need to have an overall form, a stance that harkens back to Aristotle's *Poetics*: "Now a whole is that which has a beginning, middle, and end" (Aristotle 1947, 634). Functionalists, on the other hand, focus less on the structure and more on the functions of narrative, particularly on the interaction between the narrator and the reader/listener and on how narrative is used to construct and convey meaning (Wilensky 1982; Ryan 2006). For functionalists, the boundaries of the category of narrative are determined less by the structure of the text than by the intention of the teller and the apprehension of the listener. A set of instructions on how to build a model airplane might seem far from a narrative, argues David Rudrum, but in the end whether it qualifies as narrative depends on the "use to which the text is put" (Rudrum 2005, 202). If the instructions are apprehended as a process with a beginning, a middle (with some struggle), and the possibility of a heroic ending, it might well have narrative properties.[1]

For our purposes, it is not necessary to resolve the dispute; a working definition of narrative can include both form and function. Nor is it necessary to determine precisely the boundaries of the category, of what is and is not a "story." It is more useful to focus on the archetypes at its core. Whether or not a description of the Big Bang and the origins of the universe is or is not a story may be ambiguous (Ryan 2006), but there is little doubt that "Little Red Riding Hood" fits squarely in the category. Such a strategy makes it possible to talk about the relative *narrativity* of symbolic constructs, depending on the extent to which they possess certain essential elements.

Before turning to a discussion of the core elements of narrative, let me be clear that I fully recognize the stunning diversity of forms narratives may take in different contexts and different cultures, and the multiplicity of functions narratives may serve. A Hopi creation myth is a long way from Joyce's *Ullysses*. Yet focusing on the common elements rather than on the differences is appropriate. First, just as the extraordinary variety of life arises from a simple and commonly shared genetic code, so the enormous diversity in narrative form and function is made possible by a relatively simple and commonly held narrative code. Second, most of the stories that enable us to make sense of the world, to evoke our emotions, to establish our identity, and to motivate our actions take relatively simple forms. Third, for reasons that will become clearer in subsequent chapters, the stories of greatest importance in collective action are those of popular culture, which tend to take simpler forms and are, therefore, more likely to correspond to core archetypes (Mandler and Johnson 1977). It is no accident that scholars of folklore and mythology have tended to think more in terms of commonalities of structure and function rather than of differences (Propp, Pirkova-Jakobsonova, and Scott 1958, Campbell 1968).

In a Monte Python skit parodying the news, the (faux) newscaster intones in best BBC newscaster voice (I paraphrase from memory), "A man has barricaded himself in his house. However, he is unarmed, and no one is paying any attention." When I do my (weak) impression of Monte Python's parody, my students generally chuckle (perhaps they would laugh harder if my impression were better). Why? Because they recognize immediately that this is not a story, at least not a very good one. Monte Python is playing against our concept of what a story is, particularly our conventions for news stories. Missing are the essential elements we expect in a story: plot, character, and meaning.

## Plot

Stories have a plot; a sequence of events. A story, however, is not merely events in sequence; otherwise chronologies such as a ship's log would qualify (White 1980). For Aristotle, as we have already noted, a plot must have an overall form with a beginning, a middle, and an end:

> A beginning is that which is not itself necessarily after anything else, and that has naturally something else after it; an end is that which is naturally after something itself...and with nothing else after it; and a middle, that which is by nature after one thing and has also another after it. A well constructed plot, therefore, cannot begin or end at any point one likes; beginning and end in it must be of the forms just described. (Aristotle 1947, 634)

Aristotle called this overall form its *muthos*, the Greek root for myth.

Most modern scholars of narrative have built on Aristotle. For Riessman (1993), stories have an initial *orientation* in which the context (time, place, situation, and participants) is established. There is then a *complicating action*, some event that disrupts the initial state of affairs, and creates dramatic tension. Finally there is a *resolution*, a concluding action in which the tension is resolved.[2] Turner's "dramatistic method" for interpreting social dramas has essentially the same form: an initial state of affairs, a breach, a crisis, some redress, and either reintegration or recognition of a schism (Turner 1974; Turner 1980). For Ricoeur, a plot simply involves a beginning state of affairs, a middle in which there is some reversal of fortune, and either a happy or unhappy ending (Ricoeur 1984).

Initial states of affairs tend to be good or bad, desirable or undesirable, just or unjust. Some stories begin with "all is well": Adam and Eve are in the paradise of Eden; Peter Rabbit is at home with his mother; and Frodo is living happily in the Shire. Others begin badly: the Israelites are enslaved in Egypt; Cinderella is oppressed by her stepmother; and the Ugly Duckling is, well, ugly. Then the complicating action either threatens the desirable state of affairs or offers hope of escaping the undesirable: a snake appears to tempt Eve and Adam; Moses gives hope to his people. Dramatic tension arises from uncertainty about how the story will end. Will Adam and Eve eat the apple? Will Moses and the Israelites escape? There may be many ups and downs along the way, but finally, the story ends in triumph or in tragedy, when, as Mink (1978, 238) puts it, "from the standpoint of the story it's too late to change": Adam and Eve are expelled from Eden; the Israelites reach the Promised Land.

Because stories begin with either a positive or negative initial state of affairs and—whatever twists there may be along the way—end either happily or tragically, plots are constructed from four basic prototypes.[3]

## Tragedy I: The Fall

In simple tragedy, the plot falls from good to bad, from light to dark, from life to death. Once upon a time all is well (or seems to be). Then something happens (the complicating action) to threaten the positive initial state of affairs and begin the downward movement. The action may head steadily downward, or offer moments of hope that fortunes will rise again, but in the end, the story ends badly. Figure 4.1 provides a schematic illustration of the plot of "The Fall."

The story of Adam and Eve is archetypal. In the beginning, all is well; Adam and Eve are innocents in Paradise. But then the snake tempts Eve with the apple, and the tale turns on Eve's choice. We know what follows: Eve succumbs to temptation, and then Adam. Innocence is lost. God, furious, condemns them to die and expels them from Eden.

Classic Greek tragedy shares the same plot form. As Aristotle advised, "the change of the hero's fortunes must not be from misery to happiness, but on the contrary from happiness to misery" (1947, 640). So, too, the great Shakespearian tragedies *King Lear, Macbeth, Julius Caesar*, and the rest all involve the fall of the great.

The simple tragic form provides a template for a great many stories. In popular culture, history, politics, the nightly news, autobiography, and

**The Fall**

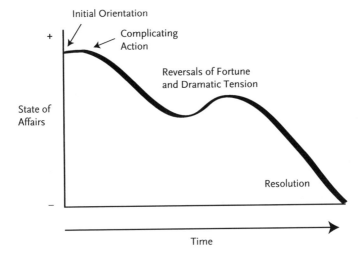

**Figure 4.1: The Fall**
Adapted from Frye (1982) and Gergen (2009)

many more contexts, a story of decline is often the vehicle for making sense of things.

## Tragedy II: Dust to Dust

A variant on simple tragedy is the plot that begins with a negative state of affairs, rises for time, but then falls back again to end badly. In the words of Ecclesiastes:

> For that which befalleth the sons of men befalleth beasts; even one thing befalleth them: as the one dieth, so dieth the other; yea, they have all one breath; so that a man hath no preeminence above a beast: for all is vanity.
>
> All go unto one place; all are of the dust, and all turn to dust again" (Ecclesiastes 3:19–20).

Figure 4.2 illustrates the rise and fall form.

The familiar story of Icarus, who escaped from prison on wings of wax, but then, not heeding the warnings of his father, flew too close to the sun and crashed to earth, is paradigmatic. Perhaps because the rise and fall shape conforms to the arc of a human life our culture holds a vast stock of

**Dust to Dust (Rise and Fall)**

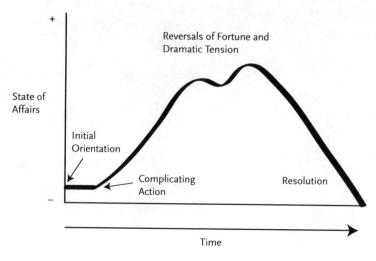

Figure 4.2: Dust to Dust (Rise and Fall)

such stories, tales of hubris, the vagaries of life, ill-fated love, or the inevitability of death.

### Triumph I: Genesis and Exodus

Not all stories end badly. A third possible plot form, therefore, begins badly but ends well, and has an overall upward movement. In these stories the plot moves from dark to light, from chaos to order, from despair to hope, from injustice to justice.

Creation myths generally take this form. In Western culture, the creation story of Genesis is archetypal. "In the beginning... the earth was without form, and void; and darkness was upon the face of the Earth." Then "God said, Let there be Light, and there was Light, and God saw the light, that it was good." And so forth for the six days of creation until, after creating man, "God saw everything that he had made, and behold, it was very good." Creation myths of other cultures display considerable variation, but themes of moving from chaos to order and from dark to light are common, and many share a similar upward arc.

Escape narratives are a second major genre in which the plot moves from bad to good. The archetypal escape narrative is Exodus, the story of Moses leading his people out of bondage in Egypt, through many trials in the

**Exodus**

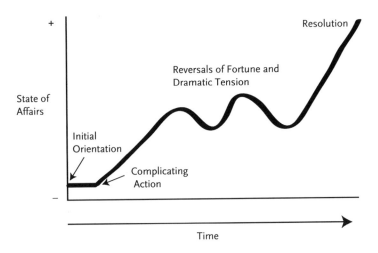

Figure 4.3: Exodus

desert, to the Promised Land. Rags-to-riches stories such as Cinderella are a variant of the escape narrative.

Creation myths, escape stories, rags-to-riches parables, and other forms of the uplifting plots are staples of historical and political narratives, as we will discuss further in subsequent chapters. The popular conception of American history, viewed as a single narrative, moves steadily upward, a story of progress, a march towards freedom. And, in politics, as Walzer (1985) has argued, Exodus holds considerable power over our collective imagination and is, therefore, central to many forms of collective action.

## Triumph II: Resurrection

The fourth plot prototype begins with a positive state of affairs, but some complicating action disrupts the status quo and the action plunges downward until there is a reversal of fortune and all ends well. This plot form is the basis of our most sacred myths, our lightest entertainments, and much in between. Moreover, as we will see, it is the form of the stories that move collective action.

Northrup Frye has argued that all fall and rise stories are symbolically about death and rebirth. Some are explicitly so. The death and resurrection of Christ is the archetype, but the Old Testament is replete with

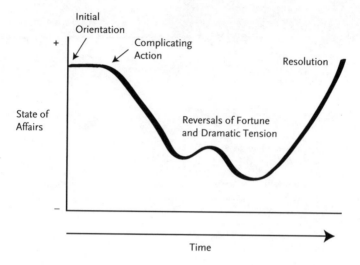

**Figure 4.4: Resurrection**

other stories of the same death and rebirth form, of descent to death or near death (symbolically hell) and restoration (symbolically heaven). Jonah and the Whale, Noah and the Arc, Daniel and the Lions' Den, and the Trials of Job: all follow the same pattern. Indeed, the entire Bible can be viewed as a single narrative with an overall fall and rise, in which, symbolically, the resurrection rescues mankind from the original sin of Adam and Eve (Frye 1982).

It is hard to overstate the ubiquity or the appeal of the resurrection plot form. Brushes-with-death stories are everywhere in folktales and popular culture. "Snow White," "Little Red Riding Hood," and "Hansel and Gretel" all involve rescue from near death. Peter Rabbit faces a near death experience in Farmer McGregor's garden, but escapes and returns safely home. One of the most watched news stories of our time was that of Jessica McClure, a baby who fell into a well and whose rescue gripped America for several days with a nearly perfect version of the resurrection archetype.

Voyage and return narratives require the hero set off on a journey in which he or she must face trials and dangers before returning to restore himself or herself and/or the community. Odysseus leaves home to fight in Troy, but then endures 20 years of trials before he finally returns to set things right in Ithaca. *The Lord of the Rings*, an amalgam of epic tropes and perhaps the most popular story of our time (rivaled now by the Harry Potter series), is an elaborate variation on the same form.

Dragon-slaying narratives are a third variant: Gilgamesh must do battle with Humbaba; David slays Goliath; Saint George kills the dragon; and Beowulf must overcome Grendel, Grendel's mother, and a dragon. In *The Hobbit*, Tolkien's light take on the genre, Bilbo trades wits with the dragon Smaug (although leaving it a more conventional hero to do the slaying) and returns a hero. (Of course, as its not-so-subtle subtitle *There and Back Again* suggests, this is also a journey narrative.) The story of the community threatened by the monster is, of course, also the formula for superhero comic books: Superman, Batman, Spiderman, and others.

This hardly exhausts the genres whose plots follow the fall and rise form. Revenge narratives, such as *The Count of Monte Christo*; comeback stories, such as *The Natural*, in which a fading baseball star recaptures a moment of old glory; and Westerns, in which order is threatened by a gang of outlaws and the lone hero rides in to restore order, all take the same form, as does lighter comedy, from Shakespeare's *All's Well That Ends Well* to the 1950s sitcom *I Love Lucy*. Our absolute favorite sports stories are about victory snatched from the jaws of defeat: the "heroic" buzzer beater, the walk-off home run, or the "Hail Mary." (For my children, growing up as Duke fans, the defining story is the "Hill-Laettner play." Look it up on YouTube.)

The template of fall and rise is the formula for hope. Perhaps this accounts for its great appeal. By coding events in this form, we can believe that the tide will turn, that a new day will dawn, that victory can still be snatched from defeat—indeed, that there is life after death.

Before turning to other key elements of narrative, let me be clear that I am not arguing that all stories fit neatly into one of these four archetypes. Literature often involves plots of enormous complexity, with multiple plot lines, stories within stories, many twists and turns, bittersweet endings, and much more. Moreover, literary stories may play against type and expectation. An ambiguous ending, for example, is bittersweet because we expect resolution to be either happy or sad. But even the most complex plots are built up from or relate to simple elements. In any event, the stories of most importance in collective action will turn out to be those that correspond more closely to the archetypes, those that have clear and simple plot lines and, as we will now explore, typecast characters.

## Character

Stories have characters, actors who make things happen or to whom things happen. Most stories involve human characters, but almost anything can be a character in stories: countries, animals, robots, viruses, ideas, the weather, and so on (Stone 1988). Usually, stories have a protagonist, a main character whose fortunes define, in large part, whether the plot is rising or falling. The term *character* also refers to the qualities of the actors, whether virtuous or venal, clever or dumb, secretive or open, and a host of other possibilities. The variety of character types is in some sense endless, but as with plots, all can be related to a limited number of basic prototypes.

Some characters are relatively passive; they are affected by the fall or rise of the plot but do not cause either.

- *Victims* are characters who suffer misfortune from falling action. Pure victims are innocent, their plight no fault of their own: the maiden taken by the dragon or polar bears starving because of global warming. These are sympathetic characters whose plight invites sorrow and anger, and whose fate we would change if we could.
- *Survivors* and other winners are sympathetic characters lifted by rising action: Cinderella rescued by the Prince or Jessica McClure pulled from the well. Their triumph brings us joy and satisfaction.

The most important characters, however, are agents whose actions drive the plot:

- *Villains* cause falling action: Judas in the Christ story or Hitler in the Holocaust. These are characters from whom we recoil and whose actions trigger anger. Villains are generally depicted as secretive, conspiratorial, greedy, dirty, cowardly, and the like.
- *Heroes*, in contrast, are agents responsible for rising action: Moses leading his people out of captivity or Lincoln saving the Union. We applaud and thrill to their triumphs. Heroes are generally depicted as open, selfless, clean, brave, and the like.

Of course, not every character neatly fits into these categories. More complex characters have elements of more than one type. As Aristotle observed, "There remains, then, the intermediate kind of personage, a man not preeminently virtuous and just, whose misfortune, however, is brought upon him not by vice or depravity but by some error of judgment" (1947, 640). Indeed, sometimes the drama lies in ambiguity of character. We do not know how *Casablanca* will end because we do not know until the end whether Rick is a rogue who will sell out the Resistance to get Ilsa, or whether, as it turns out, he is a patriot who will do the right thing at great cost to himself.

Notwithstanding the infinite variety of character, as with plot, complex characters are built up from and relate to shared expectations about the basic types. As Walter Ong (1982) has argued, stability of character and accordance with type are useful for holding stories in mind. And, also as with plot, in the popular shared stories that will be central to collective action, character tends to be painted with a broad brush, and therefore both corresponds closely to these types and maintains a stable identity throughout the story, so that it is easy to see who the victims, villains, and heroes are.

## Meaning

In addition to plot and character, stories have a point; they carry meaning. As Catherine Kohler Riessman has said, "[e]very good narrator tries to defend against the implicit accusation of a pointless story, warding off the question: 'So what?'" (Riessman 1993, 20). The meaning of a story is distinct from its form, both in its particular telling (*szujet*) and in its underlying structure (*muthos*). Its deeper meaning, or *fabula*, is the more general moral or lesson to be taken from the particular story (Bruner 1986; Kermode 2000). The fabula takes the form, "This a story about what happens when...." In *Peter Rabbit*, it is something like "the world outside is dangerous and children should heed the warnings of their parents." The fabula of the Icarus legend is that "dreamers who fly too high get burned and fall back to earth," or perhaps that "this is what happens to sons who don't listen to their fathers."[4] The meaning of a story relates to the general patterns it reveals about why things are as they are, how the world works, or what should be. As Victor Turner puts it, "[m]eaning is the only category that grasps the full relation of the part to the whole in life...." (Turner 1980, 156).

Bruner has argued that all stories involve moral judgments: "To tell a story is inescapably to take a moral stance, even if it is a moral stance against moral stances" (Bruner 1990, 51). Since plots move from good to bad or vice versa, they inevitably involve evaluation. Some stories, of course, have explicit morals, from Aesop's fables to "The Good Samaritan." In others, the moral is more ambiguous, but as long as we can tell the good guys from the bad, heroic behavior from villainous, there is a moral dimension to the story.

Meaning is not simply located in the text; it is also produced in the minds of those who read or hear it. Stories are told *by* a narrator *to* an audience (even when the audience is oneself). Audiences come to a story with expectations, assumptions, worldviews, tastes, and prior narratives. Scholars who focus on reader interpretation tend to emphasize the extent to which we bring our personal schemas to texts, and argue, therefore, that no two people get the same meaning from a story. Yet, as we will explore further in Chapter 6, to the extent that our individual interpretations of stories are enabled by a common narrative code, it is possible to have considerable convergence, and to talk, therefore, about a story's meaning for a community.

## A NOTE ON TRUTH IN NARRATIVE

All stories are fictions; some fictions are true. In my discussion of plot, character, and meaning, I have made little distinction between fiction and non-fiction. One of the most striking features of stories is that they have the same features and function in almost exactly the same way whether we believe they are "true" (i.e., non-fiction) or "untrue" (i.e., fiction). As the Nobel prize-winning economist Thomas Schelling (1983) once noted in an essay that began "Lassie died last night," when we consume fiction by watching a television program such as *Lassie*, part of our brain is aware that no real Lassie has died, indeed that there is no Lassie, only a dog or perhaps several who play Lassie, and yet still we cry. Good fiction can be no less convincing, no less compelling, than non-fiction; indeed, it is often more so (Brock and Green 2000).

Our willingness to accept the premises of a story suggests that we evaluate the truth of narrative not in terms of its precise correspondence with the real world, but in terms of its internal consistency and its conformity with our general conceptions about the way the world works. As Bruner puts it, "We interpret stories by their verisimilitude, their 'truth likeness,' or more accurately, their 'lifelikeness'" (Bruner 1990, 61).

Of course, some stories cannot be easily characterized as fiction or non-fiction. For some, the stories of the Bible are literature, for others literal truth. From a literary point of view, however, the Bible is myth, a statement which says nothing about whether it is historically true or not. Moreover, the relationship between truth and fiction is complicated. Many a truth has been conveyed by wise fictions.

## STORIES IN MIND

A clue to the centrality of narrative is the extent to which cognitive development and the development of narrative capacity are closely intertwined.

Almost as soon as children learn language, they begin to tell stories. At an extraordinarily early age, children can hold a coherent sequence of events in mind, identify agency, distinguish between what is canonical and what violates canon, and have something approximating a narrator's perspective, the key elements of narrative capacity (Bruner 1990). Julie Lynch and Paul van den Broek found that children's understandings of the conventions of narrative enabled them to make inferences about characters' goals from minimal clues (Lynch and van den Broek 2007). Children have, as Jerome Bruner (1990, 77) puts it, "the push to construct narrative."

Human cognitive development may well recapitulate our evolutionary path. The extent to which we are biologically wired for narrative has long fascinated those who have observed the ubiquity of storytelling. Scholars of mythology and folklore, most prominently Joseph Campbell, fascinated with the psychology of Freud and, especially, Jung, saw in the common structures of myth a reflection of the fundamental structure of the human mind. For Campbell, "the symbols of mythology are not manufactured; they cannot be ordered, invented or permanently suppressed. They are spontaneous productions of the psyche, and each bears within it, undamaged, the germ power of its source" (Campbell 1968, 4). Until recently, this line of thinking had largely fallen out of favor, as evolutionary biology and the humanities parted ways, but there is now a growing literature that reconnects the two.

The main insight of this scholarship is a recognition that the human brain and human culture have co-evolved. The neurobiologist Terrence Deacon (1997) has argued that language and the brain co-evolved, the cognitive neuroscientist Steven Pinker (1994) that we have an evolved "language instinct," and the evolutionary biologist Mark Pagel (2012) that we are "wired for culture."

Several scholars have made an explicit connection between our narrative capacity and human evolution. Merlin Donald (1991) has argued that there is good reason to believe that the evolution of a biological capacity for narrative separated proto-humans from modern humans. In Donald's analysis, the break came with the shift from "mimetic" culture, in which our ancestors lacked both the anatomical and intellectual ability to use language as a symbolic system, to "mythic" culture, marked by the ability to speak and to use symbolic language. For Donald, the essential purpose of this new linguistic capacity was to enable narrative. Sociobiologist E. O. Wilson has written that "[t]he mind is a narrative machine, guided unconsciously by the epigenetic rules in creating scenarios and creating options. The narratives and artifacts that prove most innately satisfying spread and become culture.... The long-term interaction of genes and culture appear

to form a cycle, or more precisely a forward traveling evolutionary spiral..."
(Wilson 2005, ix). Biologist and anthropologist David Sloan Wilson summarizes a great deal of contemporary literature on the centrality of narrative to human behavior with the observation that

> people embark upon evolutionary voyages of their own, individually and collectively, arriving at new solutions to modern problems. Furthermore, these evolutionary voyages rely fundamentally upon stories in the creation of new and untested guides to action, the retention of proven guides to action, and the all-important transmission of guides to action from one person to another. In short, stories often play the role of genes in non-genetic evolutionary processes (Wilson 2005, 35).

Whatever its genesis, though, our narrative capacity is at the heart of what it means to be human. To be human is to share a common code of narrative, a basic template of plot forms and character types, and a common way of interpreting the meaning of stories. Furthermore, it seems that we use this tool constantly, that we live storied lives. The question, then, is what work this tool of narrative might be doing. The answer is quite a lot indeed, starting with its psychological functions in mind, in enabling and structuring cognition, in triggering emotion, in forming our sense of identity, and, ultimately, in motivating and scripting our actions.

## Cognition

How we move from the cacophony of raw stimuli that bombard us to ordered understandings of our experience is truly remarkable. Narrative turns out to be a powerful cognitive tool. By translating experience into the code of story—with plot, and character, and meaning—we make the unfamiliar familiar, the chaotic orderly, and the incomprehensible meaningful. Narrative is central to many aspects of our cognition, among them how we remember, how we form understandings, and how we imbue our experience with meaning.

### Remembering

I begin with memory, because all cognition is so fundamentally dependent on the structures already held in mind. "Great is the power of memory, a fearful thing, a deep and boundless manifoldness, O my God, and this thing is the mind, and this am I myself," said St. Augustine (Augustine 1853, 196). Even what we perceive is immediately determined by what is already "in there." As Lev Vygotsky observed, "I do not merely see something round and black with two hands; I see a clock" (Vygotsky 1978, 33). And higher-level cognitive tasks such as forming understanding of events and comprehending their meaning are even more dependent on structures already held in mind.

Narrative is fundamental to memory. A first point is that we seem to remember stories better, and the better the story, the better we remember it (Thorndyke 1977). What we remember of childhood, our first job, family vacations, or school sporting events are the good stories (Kotre 1995). Teachers can help students remember a point better by telling a story to illustrate it (Noddings and Witherell 1991; Green 2004). Not everything we remember is a story, of course. With effort and practice we can remember other symbolic constructs such as lists, formulas, and names, but rote memory is harder and often needs to be aided by mnemonics, some of which have narrative properties.

A second point has to do with the relationship between schemas and narrative. As we discussed in Chapter 3, much of our memory is schematic, not literal. What is little recognized in the literature on schemas, however, is the extent to which many of our schemas are constructed by narrative. There is some irony here in that one of the seminal papers for modern schema theory, which has largely ignored narrative, is David Rumelhart's "Notes on a Schema for Stories" (Rumelhart 1975). Rumelhart's insight was that the schema of the story is a code in which a great deal of information can be stored in a single, familiar, structure. The story schema, therefore, is an excellent device for schematization about other things.

That many of our schemas are established by narrative is clearest when we think of categorical schemas such as stereotypes. The lumberjack schema of a tough, beer-drinking, flannel-shirt-wearing figure is established by the stories we tell about lumberjacks and the parts they play or could play. (Of course, we also know how to mock the stereotype, as in the Monty Python sketch in which apparently meek fellows sing "I'm a lumberjack and I'm OK....") So, too, our schemas for liberals and conservatives, for politicians and soldiers, for corporations and unions, and for all the other actors in the political landscape are established by the stories we tell about them, stories that establish the character of such actors. The narrative basis for other types of schema may be less obvious, but schemas for even complex concepts such as "appeasement" are established through stories about Chamberlain's deal with Hitler at Munich and other such tales of dealing with bullies (McDonough 2002).

The relationship between narrative and memory goes deeper still. As Bartlett (1932) first demonstrated, memory turns out to be less an act of recall than an act of reconstruction. In one of his most famous experiments, Bartlett evaluated subjects' abilities to recall a story that had been read to them. Over time, elements were both lost and gained. With each recalling, the stories became more coherent, "better" stories, with a clearer plot, more distinct characters, and heightened drama. Bartlett demonstrated that we most readily recall our "attitude" towards past events, not the actual events. We then construct a story whose point or meaning justifies our remembered attitude. What we remember, it seems, is the story that "should" have happened, not what actually did.

John Kotre (1995) discusses the famous case of John Dean, key witness in the Watergate hearings, who remembered so clearly and portrayed so vividly in his Congressional testimony the damning discussions he had had with President Nixon in the Oval Office. But when, eventually, tapes of these conversations became available, Dean's memory was shown to be quite faulty. Why the distortion? Because what Dean remembered was the "meeting as it should have been" (Kotre 1995, 51).

## Understanding

At the core of cognition is the transformation of raw perception into categorized, ordered, and comprehensible mental constructs. We are the species that looks at the stars and sees Orion the hunter. Humans do not merely experience; we seek to understand our experience, to make sense of it. As Suzanne Langer has said, "Man can adapt himself somehow to anything his imagination can cope with; but he cannot deal with Chaos" (quoted in Geertz 1973, 99).

It is no accident that the word *narrative* derives from the same root as knowing, from the Latin *gnarus* and ultimately from the Proto-Indo-European root *gnō* (White 1980). When we tell a story about the world, we take the disorder of reality and put it in the comfortable code of narrative: the familiarity of plots with beginnings, middles, and ends; of recognizable characters like heroes and villains; and of clear cause and effect. As Mink puts it, "the cognitive function of narrative form...is not just to relate a succession of events but to body forth an ensemble of relationships of many kinds of a single whole" (Mink 2001, 218). To say "I understand" something, therefore, comes very close to saying "I can tell a story in which it makes sense."

In part, understanding is about recognition and categorization, about fitting the new into something familiar. To *know*, though, often means more than categorization and association; it may also be to explain. When something happens, it's not just the *what* that concerns us, it's also the *why*. Unless we can explain, we cannot predict, and an unpredictable world would be a dangerous world indeed. When we see a bolt of lightning and hear a clap of thunder, we want to explain it, whether that explanation is that the gods are angry or that we have just witnessed the discharge of electrical energy stored in cumulonimbus clouds.

Causal explanation is a central function of narrative. In stories, events are consequences of circumstance and agency: gods are capricious, villains cause downfalls, heroes save the day. By putting our experience into stories, inevitably we are explaining *why* things happen. Usually, causality in the narratives we construct reflects our prior schemas about how things generally happen, schemas that are themselves artifacts of meta-narratives. Those with conspiratorial casts of mind tell conspiracy stories; those with negative schemas about government or politicians tell stories of incompetence or corruption; and so forth. The relentless codification of causality in narrative makes predictable an otherwise unpredictable world. As Ricoeur put it, "To make a plot is already to make the intelligible spring from the accidental, the universal from the singular, the necessary or the probable from the episodic" (Ricoeur 1984, 41).

Stories are particularly important for explaining the unusual. From infancy humans attend more closely to strange noises, new tastes or smells, and changes in routine. As we develop, our attention to the non-canonical is reflected in our storytelling. This is why stories are so often about events that disturb, surprise, frighten, or exhilarate. The usual is, literally, unremarkable. Through stories, however, we reconcile the unusual with the normal and explain the apparently inexplicable. When we put events in narrative form, we are saying, "Here is a potentially problematic action that becomes quite sensible within this set of circumstances" (Bennett 1997, 81).

The conventions of narrative enable us to infer a great deal from relatively little. Stories invite us to connect the dots. Bruner gives the example of the following simple dialogue:

"Where's Jack?"
"Well, I saw a yellow VW outside of Susan's."

Immediately the mind leaps to various narrative possibilities. Jack must be visiting Susan. Why doesn't the narrator say it outright? Is there something illicit in the visit? And so on (Bruner 1986, 27).

Umberto Eco argues that as we read or hear a story, we actively participate by writing a tentative "ghost chapter" in which we fill in missing elements of the story and anticipate the future course of events: "Given a series of causally and linearly connected events *a...e,* a text tells the reader about event *a* and, after a while, about event *e,* taking for granted that the reader has already anticipated events *b, c,* and *d*" (Eco 1984, 214). Rukmini Bhaya Nair (2002, 215) demonstrates how this works with a very simple traditional Bengali story.

> *A tiger.*
> *A hunter.*
> *A tiger.*

Just six words, but immediately the mind goes to work to fill in the blanks. In the beginning there is a tiger, a dangerous animal. A hunter arrives, the adversary of the tiger, presumably to kill the tiger. But, somehow, the tiger turns the tables on the hunter and prevails. The story has a complete plot, characters, and an ironic point.

Of course, with the ability to make large inferential leaps and to construct narratives from minimal facts comes the risk of false inferences. History is replete with widely believed falsehoods in which narratives connected the dots in wildly wrong ways. False but firmly held beliefs among some that Barack Obama was born outside the United States, that Jews were behind the World Trade Center attack, and that climate change scientists are perpetrating a hoax are all products of our propensity for spinning complete tales from few "facts," or perhaps no facts at all—tales that don't so much fit the facts as that fit with narrative schemas already in mind.

## Creating Meaning

Humans are not satisfied with just making sense of experience; we want to know its deeper *meaning.* As Roland Barthes put it, the mind "ceaselessly substitutes meaning for the straightforward copy of events recounted" (quoted in White 1981, 2). As we have discussed, the meaning of *meaning* is elusive. Here what I am interested in is the sense of the word when we say, "yes I know what happened, but what does it *really* mean?" The meaning of an event relates to its more general implications, its ultimate consequences, and the larger, more universal, narrative of which it is an episode.

Stories, as we have discussed, always have a point, a *fabula*, that relates to the larger, more universal patterns revealed by particular events. The meaning of the story "The Tortoise and the Hare" is not that "this turtle defeated that rabbit," it is that "slow and steady wins the race." When we construct stories to interpret our experience, therefore, we imbue that experience with meaning: "By using narrative form we assign meaning to events and invest them with coherence, integrity, fullness, and closure" (Gudmundsdottir 1995, 31).

Our search for meaning begins early in life. Gudmundsdottir (1995) describes an experiment by Michotte (1963) involving young children who were shown a collection of geometric shapes moving at random. Immediately, the children invented a story about what was happening: "The experiment with geometric figures involved progressing from something almost meaningless to a form endowed with meaning" (Gudmundsdottir 1995, 34). The habit of constructing stories to make experience meaningful, to move from the particular to the more general pattern it reveals, is deeply engrained. The meanings of the nightly news stories about the drunk driver involved in a fatal accident, or of a gang member pulling a knife in school, or of the politician accepting a bribe, are not in the particular, but rather in the general consequences of drinking and driving, the behavior of gang members, and the corruptibility of politicians. And, as we interpret these incidents, we also "demand that sequences of real events be assessed as to their significance as elements of a *moral* drama" (White 1980, 20, italics in the original). The point of the stories about drunk drivers, gang members, and politicians is not just that this is how such characters behave, but also that their behavior is wrong.

It is interesting to note the close parallel between the meaning-making function of narratives and the role narratives play in memory. As Shore puts it, "[t]he experience of something new becoming meaningful is similar to the experience of remembering something long-forgotten but recovered in memory" (1996, 326). Both making meaning and remembering are acts of narrative construction, an effort to put experience in the form of a story that must be or have been. And the meaning-making function of narrative is in some sense the mirror image of its sense-making function. When we use narrative to make sense, we are constructing a particular story on the basis of our general worldview. When we use narrative to make meaning, on the other hand, we are reinforcing our general worldview through the particular.

Humans not only think, we also feel. We love and hate, hope and fear, rejoice and grieve, pity and envy, lust and recoil, and much more. Although our emotions clearly color our thinking and affect our behavior, there is little consensus about how this works. Indeed, there not even agreement on a list of emotions. As Theodore Sarbin reports, "Aristotle identified fifteen [emotions], Descartes six, Hobbes proposed seven. McDougall also offered a list of seven. More recently, Plutchik identified eight primary emotions, Tompkins nine" (Sarbin 2001, 218). There are almost as many schools of thought about the nature and function of emotion. The *Stanford Encyclopedia of Philosophy*, in answering the question, "What are emotions?" concludes that they "might be physiological processes, or perceptions of physiological processes, or neuro-psychological states, or adaptive dispositions, or evaluative judgments, or computational states, or even social facts or dynamical processes," or all of the above (de Souza 2013).

The relationship between emotion and narrative is not emphasized in the psychological literature. Yet emotion is closely related to narrative. Certainly stories can trigger emotion, a phenomenon with which we are all familiar. But before turning to the question of how stories evoke emotional responses, on which the next chapter will focus, here I want to suggest that our emotions are in some ways inseparable from narrative, that they are, as Sarbin has called them, "narrative emplotments": "Instances of emotional life, shame, guilt, anger, pride, and other so-called "emotions," are more parsimoniously construed as narrative plots" (Sarbin 2001, 217). Love, then, can be defined as a deep desire that another's story end well, hate that a villain gets his just reward, anger a response to a narrative of injustice, fear that a sympathetic protagonist's (or one's own) story may end badly, and hope that it might yet end well. In this line of thought, emotions are affective stances coded by narrative in the mind.

The reason stories trigger emotion, therefore, is that they so closely simulate how we process all emotions. But the relationship between narrative and emotion could and likely does also go the other way: emotions prompt us to construct stories that justify and explain our feelings. When we are angry at someone, for whatever reason, we are more likely to construct stories that justify that emotional stance, more likely to accept negative stories about that person, and more likely to recall stories that cast the person in a bad light. Conversely, when we love, we construct, accept, and remember positive stories. What appears to be going on here is that we are constructing the story whose point reinforces our affective stance. This phenomenon can be seen clearly in conflict situations in which narratives of other are used to justify fear and hatred. In the Jim Crow South, for example, stories about rapes by black men (Dittmer 1977), or in 18th- and early 19th-century America, about savage acts by Native Americans (Slotkin 1973), were vehicles for justifying racist attitudes and actions.

The foregoing discussion of affect and narrative has treated emotion as something quite distinct from cognition, which is consistent with what was once the dominant approach in psychology. However, there is a grow- ing body of literature demonstrating how emotion and cognition interact (Forgas 1995; Mayer and Salovey 1995; Lerner and Keltner 2000; Forgas and George 2001, Dunn and Schweitzer 2005; Forgas 2008). Bower and Cohen document the impact of emotion on memory, perception, judg- ment, and thinking: "A person's feelings act like a selective filter that is tuned to incoming material that supports or justifies those feelings" and "affect what records they can retrieve from memory" (Bower and Cohen 1982, 291).

Whether emotion assists or distorts cognition is a matter of some debate. On the one hand, we know that emotion can cloud reason, which is why it has often been viewed as something to be overcome. On the other hand, emotion can assist cognition by directing our attention and storing in memory only those things that are truly important (de Sousa 1987). George Marcus and colleagues apply this line of thought to political rea- soning, arguing that emotions enable us to attend to politics only when needed, and that "emotion and reason interact to produce a thoughtful and attentive citizenry" (Marcus, Neuman, and MacKuen 2000, 1). This seems too sanguine, however. Emotion, while functional in many respects, can also be quite dysfunctional. Like many evolved characteristics that are adaptive in some contexts—our taste for sweets, for example—the impact of our emotions on cognition can be maladaptive in others, most nota- bly when false narratives trigger inappropriate emotional responses, and vice versa.

## IDENTITY

Humans seek not only to understand, not only to find meaning, but also to know who we are and to locate ourselves in the world. To ask, "Who am I?" is a basic human impulse. Narrative is a fundamental tool for establish- ing our identity. That our experience of our own life is "storied" has been explored by many scholars, among them Erving Goffmann (1959), Alasdair MacIntyre (1981), Dan McAdams (1997), Theodore Sarbin (2001), and Jerome Bruner (2004). As Bruner puts it, "we become the autobiographical narratives by which we 'tell about' our lives" (Bruner 2004). When called upon to answer "Who are you?" to another, or "Who am I" to oneself, the answer is always a story.

Identity requires, first, self-awareness: the ability to see oneself, not a simple proposition. As Mead put it,

> The individual experiences himself as such, not directly, but only indirectly, from the standpoints of other individual members of the same social group or from the generalized standpoint of the social group as a whole to which he belongs. For he enters his own experience as a self or an individual not directly or immediately, but only insofar as he first becomes an object to himself just as other individuals are objects to him or are in his experience; and he becomes an object to himself only by taking the attitudes of other individuals toward himself within a social environment or context of experience and behavior in which both he and they are involved. (Mead 1934, 203)

Self-awareness, therefore, requires adopting the position of another with respect to oneself.

Narrative is particularly well suited to this task. When we tell a story about ourselves, we cast ourselves as actors in that narrative and see ourselves as others might. As David Carr puts it, "We are constantly striving, with more or less success, to occupy the storyteller's position with respect to our own lives" (Carr 1997, 16). By situating our actions in story, we put them in a form that can be understood by others, as well as by ourselves (Goffman 1959, Taylor 1992). The development of self-awareness in children appears to be enabled by learning to tell stories about themselves. When children are very young, parents and other caregivers tell stories about them in their presence. By the age of three or so, children begin collaborating in the telling (Miller, Potts, Fung, Hoogstra, and Mintz 1990). This, then, is the beginning of the autobiographical narrative capacity of our mature lives.

Stories do more than create self-awareness, they also establish what kind of character we are. As Kotre puts it, "The work done by our autobiographical memory system is aimed at establishing the main character in our story" (Kotre 1995, 120). Particular stories stand out in memory. Some are pivotal in the plot of our life story. We remember the discovery of a talent that would lead to our future success, the break that got us started on our career or (less happily) began the downward slide. Alcoholics will often remember their first drink (Kotre 1995, 211). Other stories are remembered because they seem to reveal the essence of our character. Kotre tells the story of a man who has skimped on scuba diving equipment. When it fails during a dive, and he thinks he is drowning, the incident becomes emblematic of the larger pattern of his life: " 'I've been a tightwad all my life and now I'm going to pay for it' " (Kotre 1995, 120).

Our autobiographical memory is at once episodic and coherent. The particular stories of our life can be arrayed into a more or less coherent single narrative. Together these stories establish our character through the roles we have played in the drama of our life to date, and, importantly, define the roles we might appropriately play in the future. Often we cast our self as the hero of our personal narrative, as the agent responsible for our successes and triumphs. If MacIntyre is right that human life is a "narrated quest," then it seems we are intent on being the hero of that epic (MacIntyre 1997, 257). Not all life stories are triumphant, of course. The story may be tragic—of potential never reached, opportunity squandered, or failure in work or love. In these tragedies, typically, we cast ourselves as the victim and not the villain. "I could have been a contender," bemoans Marlon Brando in *On the Waterfront*. Of course, there are innumerable variations on the hero and victim archetypes, but these do seem to be extremely common basic orientations, as Goffman found in his work on mental illness:

> If the person can manage to present a view of his current situation which shows the operation of favourable personal qualities in the past and a favourable destiny awaiting him, it may be called a success story. If the facts of a person's past and present are extremely dismal, then about the best he can do is to show that he is not responsible for what has become of him, and the term sad tale is appropriate. (Goffman 1976, 248)

We are constantly at work revising and improving our life's narrative. Like Bartlett's subjects in his memory experiments, details that detract from the story fall away and new details are added, all in service of improving the narrative line. Particular events are transformed into generic and timeless stories, often introduced by the phrase "We used to..." When the autobiographical system has done its job, we are left with a kind of mythologized autobiography. "As maker of myth, the self leaves its handiwork everywhere in memory," writes Kotre (1995, 117). Among the functions of our self-mythologizing is the ability to see our lives as a coherent whole (McAdams 1997). By narrativizing our autobiographies we inevitably give meaning to them. Such is the nature of stories; they have a point. The stories of our life, therefore, not only answer the question "Who am I?" but also enable us to see our lives as meaningful.

Autobiographical narratives also serve to maintain a sense of continuity of character, a sense that we are the same person over time. For Douglas Ezzy, "A narrative identity provides a subjective sense of self-continuity as it symbolically integrates the events of lived experience in the plot of the story a person tells about his or her life" (Ezzy 1998, 239). Maintaining our character's integrity appears to be of considerable psychological importance. Paul Ricoeur notes that there are two common meanings of the term "identity," one of which we have been discussing, the other of which is "sameness" (Ricoeur 1991, 73). Both turn out to be important. We want to establish not only who we are, but also that we are the same person over time. Integrity of character makes us more predictable to others and to ourselves, and thereby simplifies the problem of knowing what to do.

Maintaining our life narrative is a constant challenge, rarely a settled matter. Our life stories are often fragmented, commonly threaten to change or disappear, and very often are still unfolding. As a consequence, "[n]arrative identities are very much in-process and unfinished, continuously made and remade as episodes happen" (Cam 1985, quoted in Ezzy 1998, 247). Indeed, there is always the threat that we will lose the narrative thread altogether, and with it our sense of identity and purpose in life. We are, therefore, always at work constructing the stories that tell us who we are and what the point of our life might be.

## ACTING

By now, it is no doubt abundantly clear where I am going with this argument: much of human behavior is acting. The word *acting* has multiple meanings in common use, as Victor Turner has explored (1974, 102). It is sometimes synonymous with unselfconscious behavior (driving to work, for example). It can also mean the pretense of appearing to do one thing, while actually doing another (feigning innocence when caught with our hand in the cookie jar). But the sense in which I want to use acting comes closest to that of performance on stage, acting in its dramatic sense.

The metaphor of life as drama has a fine pedigree that goes back at least to Shakespeare: "All the world's a stage, and all the men and women merely players" (Shakespeare 1998, 151). For Bruner, "When we enter human life, it is as if we walked on stage into a play whose enactment is already in progress—a play whose somewhat open plot determines what parts we may play and towards what denouements we may be heading" (Bruner 1990, 34). The stage metaphor suggests that we are not just audience but players in and, perhaps, authors of the story of our lives.

MacIntyre's concept of an "intelligible act" and Bruner's similar concept of an "act of meaning" provide useful starting points for making sense of the proposition that much of human action is narrative enactment. MacIntyre argues that for an act to be intelligible to others and to ourselves, it must be possible to say what it is that we are doing.

> To identify an occurrence as an action is in the paradigmatic instances to identify it under a type of description which enables us to see that occurrence as flowing intelligibly from a human agent's intentions, motives, passions, and purposes. It is therefore to understand an action as something for which someone is accountable, about which it is always appropriate to ask the agent for an intelligible account. (MacIntyre 1997, 247)

An action is intelligible if we can tell a story in which it makes sense given the character of the actor and the circumstances in which she finds herself. Similarly, for Bruner, an "act of meaning" is an action for which we can tell a meaningful story. The crucial point is that humans do not just use narrative to make our actions intelligible or meaningful; we act in ways that *are* intelligible and meaningful, that make sense in some narrative. We anticipate that we will be held to account by others or by ourselves to explain what it is we are doing. To act intelligibly or meaningfully is to anticipate the need to justify one's actions through story.

But there is another sense in which, as Bruner puts it, "[t]he Self as narrator not only recounts but justifies" (Bruner 1990, 121). We are not only interested in being understood, we also care about being approved of, about being able to say that we did the right thing. As I have argued, narrative almost inevitably carries with it a normative undertone, a moral stance. When we enact narrative, we just as inevitability seek to cast ourselves as acting appropriately, legitimately, and morally. And as with intelligibility, we not only use narrative to justify our actions, we act in ways that can be justified by a story in which our character did the right thing. We anticipate the moral of the narrative in which our actions will be interpreted, anticipate being held to account for the moral implications of our actions.

The narrative integrity of our autobiographical ambitions demands certain actions and precludes others. Our sense of self, the leading character in the dramatic sweep of our lives, lays out those behaviors that are explicable, meaningful, and justifiable given the circumstances in which we find ourselves. Not that we aren't tempted and that we don't fail, but we can nonetheless be called to conduct that maintains the integrity of our character in the narrative we are writing. As Jon Elster (1989, 201) has commented, "If one can say to oneself: 'I am not the kind of person who yields to temptation,' it becomes easier to resist."

And there is yet one more way in which our actions are driven by the dramatic demands of narrative. We can be driven by the desire to script a happy ending and to cast ourselves as the hero in the epic of our lives. For some, life as MacIntyre put it, is a "narrated quest" in which they long to play the hero so much that they will act the part. Why climb Mount Everest? Because it is, in dramatic terms, an epic battle of human against nature, of life against death, and because reaching the summit is the ultimate dramatic triumph. In the words of one climber, "I thought I saw in the vision of success [on the mountain] a wonderful meaning to life—my triumph over the gross materialism in which our civilization as I knew it had been plunged" (Ortner 1999, 37).

We are moved to act by the dramatic imperatives of our personal narratives. Not all of our actions are so motivated—we are, after all, also creatures of calculation and habit—but we are also, fundamentally, enactors of stories, deeply desirous that our life story ring true, that it will cohere, that it will have a point, and that it will end well. And, as we will explore in the next chapter, because we are the storytelling animal, we can be called to act by the stories told to us.

# CHAPTER 5

# The Call of Stories

*There is no Frigate like a Book*
*To take us Lands away*
*Nor any Coursers like a Page*
*Of Prancing Poetry*
Emily Dickinson (1961, 724)

*How selfish soever man may be supposed, there are evidently some principles in his nature, which interest him in the fortune of others, and render their happiness necessary to him, though he derives nothing from it except the pleasure of seeing it.*
Adam Smith (1969, 47)

In the last chapter I argued that humans are essentially storytelling animals. My focus was on narrative as an empowering and enabling tool *of* mind, on the role of stories in cognition, emotion, identity, and action. I turn now to the power of narrative *on* mind, what Coles has called the "call of stories," the impact of stories told to us by others (Coles 1989).

The power of stories is not news to those whose business is persuasion. Charities soliciting contributions, preachers seeking converts, advertisers selling products, politicians soliciting votes, generals stirring their troops, coaches recruiting players, and leaders inspiring followers: all tell stories. They believe that as creatures constituted by narrative, we can be moved by narrative.

In this chapter I explore why, when, and how it is that stories told by others move us. I consider, first, the phenomenon of *engrossment*, the experience of "losing ourselves" in a story. Engrossing stories capture our minds and stir our passions. I then explore how stories that engross can persuade, by altering our attitudes, changing our beliefs, and constructing our interests. Moreover, they can so frame an issue that acting becomes an expression of identity and, indeed, a moral imperative.

## ENGROSSMENT: HOW STORIES CAPTURE OUR MINDS AND STIR OUR PASSIONS

We are all aware that stories can capture us. I have work to do in the evening, but I just finished the second of Stieg Larsson's Millennium series, and the third beckons. Just a few minutes couldn't hurt, but I start reading, and soon I'm caught up again in the tangled tale of Lisbeth Salander, and hours later I ruefully come back to the reality that my work is still undone. (I am not alone. As a reviewer put it, "Anyone who has succumbed to Larsson fever knows what it is to lavish the waking hours of entire weekends on his weirdly matter-of-fact and even more weirdly addictive fiction, surfacing at the end of the binge, bleary-eyed and underfed, wondering what just happened" (Miller 2010). Stories are seductive.

What happens when we are pulled into a story? In the grip of a good novel, awareness of everything else slips away: thoughts of job or school, the sounds of cars passing on the street, the image of the book itself and of the room where we sit all recede from consciousness. Indeed, time itself is suspended. Nel Noddings (1984) calls the phenomenon "engrossment." Victor Nell (1988) describes how a reader can become "lost in the story." Richard Gerrig uses the term "transportation," comparing engrossment to the experience of traveling to another place (Gerrig 1993). As with literal transportation, when we travel to the world created by the story, "parts of the world of origin become inaccessible...." (Brock and Green 2000, 702). Transportation is a "convergent process" in which "all mental processes and capacities become focused on events occurring in the narrative" (Brock and Green 2000, 701). The phenomenon can also be thought of as a form or what Mihaly Csikszentmihalyi (1997) has called "flow," a state of heightened focus and immersion we experience in art, play, and work.

When we are engrossed in a story, we accept its premises. It seems perfectly normal that "hobbits" talk with "wizards," boys draw magic swords from stones, and girls have fairy godmothers. Stories, good ones anyway, allow us to accept even the strangest of premises as long as the conventions of narrative are followed.

When engrossed, we may identify with characters in the story and imagine ourselves in their situation. Stories, argues Bruner, enable us to "leap through the proscenium to become (if only for a moment) whoever is on stage in whatever plight they may find themselves" (1990, 54). When we read *Huckleberry Finn*, we become Huck for a time, floating on that raft with Jim, watching the shore drift by (Coles 1989, 35). When we identify with characters, we experience what (we imagine) they are experiencing, we feel their fear, their sadness, their excitement, their hopes.

Stories that capture our minds also arouse our passions; we *care* about what happens to the characters. We fall in love with Ilsa (or Rick) in *Casablanca*, we exalt in Frodo's triumph in Tolkien's epic, we cry for Celie in *The Color Purple*, we pity Oedipus, wishing there was some escape from the unfolding tragedy. Once, on a transcontinental flight, I found myself holding back a tear of joy for Shrek, a cartoon ogre in a movie I had not intended to watch. Of course, stories we believe to be true have power, too. Consider our emotional responses to the stories about 9/11. We felt fury at the hijackers, fear that there could be other attacks, pity for the victims in the World Trade Center, compassion for the families searching for missing sons and daughters, pride in the response of the rescuers, and awe at the courage of the passengers on United Flight 93.

It is curious that knowing that a story is "fiction" has little impact on our emotional responses. Schelling puzzles over an episode of the old television show *Lassie*:

> Lassie died one night. Millions of people, not all of them children, grieved. At least they shed tears. Except for the youngest, the mourners knew that Lassie didn't really exist. Whatever that means. Perhaps with their left hemispheres they could articulate that they had been watching a trained dog, and that *that* dog was still alive, healthy and rich; meanwhile in their right hemispheres, or some such place (if these phenomena have a place) the real Lassie had died. (Schelling 1983, 179)

Although we experience stories somewhat differently from real life—for example, we are less likely to experience primary emotions such as sadness and anger when reading than in real life (Miall and Kuiken 2002)—and part of our brain knows that we can pop out of the story if the horror movie gets too intense, it is striking is just how similar our emotional responses are to fiction and non-fiction. As Jeanne Deslandes argues, "Emoting is not predicated upon the empiric reality of the stimulus" (Deslandes 2004, 355).

Some scholars have argued that emotional responses to fictions cannot be genuine. But emotion and narrative are so deeply entangled, as we discussed in the previous chapter, that when we enter a story such as *Lassie* and imagine ourselves in the position of Timmie, Lassie's owner, we feel genuine sorrow because the story is a tragedy, because it takes the narrative form in which the emotion "sorrow" is encoded. Indeed, turning the puzzle on its head, one could argue that events known to be real only have emotional impact when they are made into a story. The movie *Titanic* adds nothing to our knowledge that a ship sank and many died, but by weaving the events into a dramatic story, with sympathetic characters, heroes, and villains, the movie has a much more profound impact on us.

There remains a puzzle, however, as to how we become engrossed. As Kieren Egan asks, "Why is a child so engrossed by a story about a rabbit who wears a nice blue coat and is given cups of Chamomile tea by his mother?"(Egan 1995, 120). In part, engrossment depends on our active engagement with a story. Gerrig (1993) cites a passage from Stephen Oates' biography of Lincoln, *With Malice Towards None*. Mary and Abraham Lincoln are deciding whether or not to go to Ford's theater. They don't really want to go, but they have promised to attend and the newspapers have announced that they would be there. Gerrig argues that the story engages us as participants in two ways. First, the story requires that we bring considerable knowledge to the story and, without being aware of doing so, we work to fill in the gaps (which, of course, the author expects). We understand that presidents are supposed to keep promises, that the newspapers would print certain stories if the president didn't show, and that there would likely be political consequences to those stories. We may know something of Lincoln's relationship with his wife and imagine a conversation they might have had. The more a story engages our prior knowledge and schemas, Gerrig argues, the more transported we are likely to be.

We also find ourselves engaged in the story's unfolding plot. We know that Lincoln is in danger; if he goes to the theater he will be shot. There is no way to read the story without hearing a voice crying out "Don't go to the theater!" (Gerrig 1993, 176). We actively imagine how the story might go from here, fearing for the worst and hoping for the best. We imagine the story that might have been if the Lincolns had not promised to attend, if their attendance had not been publicized, and so forth. Gerrig terms this tendency *anomalous replotting*: "actively thinking about what could have happened to change an outcome" (1993, 177).

Why does this engagement lead to engrossment? One interpretation is that narratives mimic real experience, that stories create virtual experiences with many of the same properties as the real thing. Perhaps a better way to interpret what is going on when we are engrossed is not that we confuse narrative reality with the "real" thing, but rather that our "normal" experience of reality is so deeply narrativized that when we enter a story we are substituting one narrative reality for another. Stories engross us because they are in the same code as our normal consciousness; they have the same form as our constructed reality.

## PERSUASION

Persuasion involves a change in attitudes, beliefs, or interests. So defined, persuasion can be distinguished both from coercion, in which threats alter payoffs without changing underlying motives, and from manipulation, in which the dimensions of choice are constrained (Riker 1984). How are we persuaded by others? Certainly new information and reasoned argument can persuade. If I learn that paper bags use more energy to produce than plastic bags, I may change my beliefs about which is better for the environment. All else being equal, "people want to have correct attitudes and beliefs, since these will normally prove to be most helpful in dealing with everyday problems" (Petty, Cacioppo, Strathman, and Priester 1994, 115). Although "correct" attitudes and beliefs may be useful, arriving at them is hard because it is costly to acquire and process information (Downs 1957). It is no surprise, therefore, that we are often persuaded not by fact but by narrative. Stories that capture our minds can alter our attitudes, transform our beliefs, and construct our interests.

### Attitudes

Narratives can persuade by establishing or altering attitudes towards persons or other entities. An "attitude is a psychological tendency that is expressed by evaluating a particular entity with some degree of favor or disfavor" (Eagly and Chaiken 1993, 1). Attitudes are, therefore, essentially general affective stances stored in memory. Given what we know about the emotive power of stories, it is not surprising that stories might be capable of establishing and altering attitudes. Engrossed in a story, we are compelled to adopt an emotional stance towards the characters in them, to pity the victim, to admire the hero, to loath the villain. A lasting impact of such stories is our feelings about the characters in them. Indeed, that affective or evaluative stance is what we remember best, as Bartlett (1932) demonstrated long ago.

The ability of stories to affect attitudes is well known to marketers. In a recent advertising campaign for Snickers® candy bars, a young man becomes a complaining diva (played by Aretha Franklin) because he's hungry. Upon eating the candy bar, he returns to himself. The punchline: "You're not you when you're hungry. Snickers satisfies." In 30 seconds, the ad creates positive affect by casting the candy bar as the hero rescuing the victim from hunger. Craig Thompson (1997) argues that consumers interpret their consumption through narrative and suggests the implications for marketing. Experimental evidence demonstrates the effectiveness of such narrative techniques. Baba Shiv and Joel Huber (2000) establish that providing narrative cues that enable subjects to imagine their anticipated satisfaction with a product has a significant impact on their preferences. Jennifer Escalas (2004) shows that that transportation into narrative leads to more positive attitudes towards products. Dunlop and colleagues report a similar finding with narratives intended to convey health messages (Dunlop, Wakefield, and Kashima 2010, 133).

Narratives can also affect political attitudes. A classic example is the impact of stories on American attitudes towards individuals with AIDS. In the first years after the discovery of AIDS, the prevailing narratives involved stories in which AIDS sufferers were generally portrayed unsympathetically as drug addicts or promiscuous homosexuals who were complicit in their own plight (and therefore both victim and villain). The story of Ryan White changed attitudes (Johnson 1990). White was a young boy who had contracted HIV through blood transfusions. When his school barred him from school, he and his parents protested, and the story took off. White became a national celebrity, appearing on morning television shows, in *Time* and *Newsweek* articles, and eventually a popular movie.

White's story reframed the issue and compelled a different attitude towards the disease. Here the victim was innocent, the villains were the disease and prejudice against those suffering from it, and the protagonist's (anticipated) death was a clear tragedy. It was almost impossible not to feel sympathy for White and to root for him. Other stories followed, most notably perhaps that of the immensely popular professional basketball player Magic Johnson, a hero to many, who contracted HIV through heterosexual contact, and was, therefore, an "innocent" victim as well (Langer, Zimmerman, Hendershot, and Singh 1992).[1] Together, these stories and thousands more changed attitudes about AIDS.

## Beliefs

As we explored in the last chapter, humans rely heavily on narrative to form their understanding of the world. It should not be surprising, therefore, that narratives that engross us might affect our beliefs. Narrative's impact on belief may be indirect, through attitude change, since our interpretations are strongly affected by our attitudes. But narrative can also affect beliefs by exploiting our tendency to accept the premises of a story in which we are engrossed and our predilection for narrative inference.

Experimental evidence supports this proposition. Timothy Brock and Melanie Green (2000) demonstrate that exposure to a narrative with implicit messages about the world affects beliefs and that the greater the degree of engrossment (transportation), the greater the impact. "Highly transported participants showed beliefs more consonant with story conclusions," they report (2000, 707). They speculate that "[u]nder high transportation, the individual may be distanced temporarily from current and previous schemas and experiences" (2000, 702). Whether such impacts persist may depend on how often the story is repeated.

Evidence from non-experimental settings also demonstrates the role of narrative in belief formation. Jury trials are one such venue. Bennett (1997) offers a compelling analysis of the process jurors go through in making judgments. A crime has been committed and a defendant stands accused. The evidence is confusing and contradictory. How do prosecutor and defense attorney seek to persuade the jurors? By spinning stories that incorporate the established "facts" in ways that advance their case. The prosecutor tells a tale of the vengeful wife, an unremorseful and violent character who plotted to kill her unsuspecting husband. The defense counters with a story of the abused spouse acting in self-defense, in which the husband is the villain, the wife the victim, the killing justified. How do jurors make sense of the conflicting testimony? Not, Bennett argues, through analytic reasoning but by assessing the plausibility of the stories they hear, an assessment that depends on whether the story hangs together and whether it resonates with their prior schema about how such characters would act in such circumstances. Bennett concludes that "adjudicators, like most other story audiences, judge the plausibility of a story according to certain structural relations among chosen symbols, not according to direct perception of the actual events in question" (Bennett 1997, 97).

Similar processes determine many political beliefs. Faced with the shocking attacks of 9/11, for example, Americans struggled to make sense of what had just happened. As Entman (2003) demonstrates, several interpretations were possible. One possibility was that the attacks were an isolated event by a band of terrorists, essentially a horrific crime. But President Bush and his administration chose to frame the event as an act of war, a framing that demanded a military, not a police, response. Entman argues that this frame had tremendous power in shaping media coverage in the United States, and, therefore, public understanding. What is going on here is placing the inexplicable events of that day in the context of a story in which it makes sense, a story in which a vast global conspiracy of terror-ists declared war on America. And, as I will discuss further in Chapter 6, both because the advantages of the bully pulpit gave Bush preeminence as the interpreter-in-chief and because the counter-narrative in which a small band of clever terrorists did the deed fit less well with prior narra-tives about attacks of this scale (Pearl Harbor), the war frame prevailed.[2]

Beliefs about a great many other issues in politics are also shaped by nar-ratives subscribed to by segments of the population. This is clearest with demonstrably false stories: the "birther" narrative, in which Barack Obama was born in Kenya;[3] the "death panel" narrative in which Obama's health care plans would empower bureaucrats to "pull the plug on grandma" (Krugman 2008); and the climate hoax narrative in which Al Gore, the United Nations, and liberal scientists are conspiring to limit personal free-dom (Mayer 2011). But even "true" beliefs are often established by story. What do most of us really know about climate change other than what we learn from the stories we read or hear?

Particular stories can establish, alter, or reinforce more general world-views. As we discussed in Chapter 4, the meaning of a story lies not in its particulars, but in the meta-narrative it references (its *fabula*). Ronald Reagan, for example, used the story of the "welfare queen":

> She has eighty names, thirty addresses, twelve Social Security cards and is col-lecting veteran's benefits on four non-existing deceased husbands. And she is collecting Social Security on her cards. She's got Medicaid, getting food stamps, and she is collecting welfare under each of her names. Her tax-free cash income is over $150,000. (*New York Times* 1976, 51)

The point of the story was clear: welfare is coddling those who don't deserve it. In this regard, the deeper meaning of the particular story is established by its resonance with a meta-narrative in which government programs reward laziness and create dependence, a core ideological narra-tive of contemporary American conservatism, as I will discuss further in the next chapter.

It is worth noting that even when labeled "fiction," stories can alter beliefs. In Brock and Green's (2000) experiments, impacts on belief were unaffected by whether the story was described as fiction or non-fiction to the subjects. Ayn Rand's novels, in which govern-ment and freeloaders cripple the economy, have been enormously influential among conservative thinkers in structuring a worldview in which society is divided into those who produce and those who do not ("makers" and "takers" in the popular shorthand), and in establishing anti-government and pro–free-market ideologies (Burns 2009, Heller 2009). What matters with these fictions is not whether the events are seen as factual, but whether the meaning of the story "rings true" in its essentials (Strange 2002).

### Interests

Most importantly, certainly from the standpoint of collective action, narratives can construct our interests. Interests are typically taken as given by social scientists. Yet even interests based on fundamental egoistic desires for security, power, or wealth may be partially constructed. And clearly our non-egoistic interests—in the fate of others we care about, in causes that move us, or in the fortunes of the community of which we are a member—are largely constructed. Narrative can play a role in each case.

In part, narrative's role in constructing interests is through its impact on beliefs. If we come to believe that trade agreements put our job at risk, or that violent video games lead to criminal behavior, or that attending the best preschool is essential for success in life, we may come to have an "interest" in opposing free trade, in regulating video games, or in getting our child into the elite preschool. Incorrect beliefs established by false narratives—that "Obamacare" would create "death panels," for example—can lead to an "interest" in a policy that would actually be harmful. But narrative can also affect interests more directly.

Even simple material interests can be established by narrative. This proposition is obviously true in the multi-billion dollar market for narrative itself, in the form of virtually all our entertainments, from movies to video games. Our demand for other products is greatly impacted by narratives as well. As the marketing literature demonstrates, narratives can create demand for products (Shiv and Huber 2000, Escalas 2004). Demand for diamond engagement rings, for example, can only be understood as a function of the symbolic meaning of such emblems in the context of conventional narratives about love, engagement, and marriage (Mayer 1998). The demand for an antique often depends on its "provenance," the story that accompanies it. A Confederate cavalry sword once worn by Jeb Stuart (the dashing Civil War cavalry leader) would be worth a great deal more than one that wasn't. Why? Because it is the story, not the sword, that actually creates the value.

Our primary concern here, however, is not with egoistic material interests but with those interests that are most closely connected to collective action, notably altruistic, ideological, and patriotic interests. These interests present puzzles precisely because they cannot be predicted by material circumstance. They are all, fundamentally, constructed, and, they are often, perhaps even always, constructed by narrative.

## Altruistic Interests

Clearly, humans have altruistic interests. As Adam Smith observed long ago, we are interested in the "fortune of others." We care about victims of hurricanes, children in need of foster care, and miners trapped underground. We feel pain when they are harmed, joy when they are helped. But the source of such interests is less clear. As discussed in Chapter 3, much of the literature on the origins of human altruism treats altruism as a form of reciprocity and explores how biological instincts for and/or social norms of reciprocity might have evolved. An exclusive focus on reciprocity, however, leaves out many forms of altruistic behavior and fails to explain why a predilection for altruism might be evoked in some circumstances and not in others.

Humans can be altruistic even when there is no prospect of reciprocity. Robert Frank (1988) cites the example of Lenny Skutnik, a bystander who famously jumped into the Potomac River to rescue passengers in danger of drowning in the frigid waters after their plane crashed in a snowstorm. Clearly, Skutnik could not have expected his actions to be reciprocated by those he saved. It takes little effort to think of innumerable other acts of non-reciprocated generosity, towards our children, members of our community, and even strangers. We can be "Good Samaritans."

Narrative constructs altruistic interests by creating empathy for characters in stories that engross us. In 1987, an 18-month-old girl fell into a well in Midland, Texas. For three days, as Jessica McClure's life hung in the balance and rescue workers raced to get her out, America, it seemed, couldn't get enough of the "Baby Jessica" story. CNN went into 24-hour coverage. The story was in many ways a perfect tale: an innocent victim, a fall from light into darkness (literally and figuratively), tragedy or triumph hanging in the balance, and the possibility of heroic resurrection. Why did Americans care so deeply about Jessica's fate? Because, engrossed in the gripping drama, we not only imagined what her parents might be feeling, but we also became her parents; we not only imagined the grief they would feel if their child died and the joy if she were saved, but we also anticipated the grief or joy we would feel. As President Reagan reportedly said, "everybody in America became godfathers and godmothers of Jessica while this was going on" (Thomas and Annin 1997, 34–35).

Remarkably, for many years the role of stories in altruism was largely ignored. The chapter on altruism in the *Handbook of Psychology*, for example, makes no mention of narrative (Batson and Powell 2003). Yet, those who seek to elicit altruism commonly tell stories. Consider, for example, the website of Save the Children, one of the world's largest charities. Prominent on the front page (as of April 2010) is a photograph of a young girl with the caption "Meet Carina, our 13-year-old Haiti Hope Child." A click leads to her story:

> Minutes after the earthquake struck on January 12, 2010, Carina and her family were homeless. Her little brother, Achelley, was pulled from under the rubble of their house with head injuries and respiratory problems.

Immediately, we are drawn into her story: a young girl living with a family, the horror of the earthquake, the rescue of her brother, and the magnitude of his injuries. From these bare scraps we construct a plot and cast the characters. We imagine the ways in which the story might proceed from here. Will she find a place to stay? What will happen to her family? Will her brother survive? And as soon as our narrative capacity is engaged, we start to care. We can't help ourselves. Conveniently, a link lets you become a "Haiti Hope Child sponsor for only $19 a month," suggesting that it is in your power to make the story end well, that you can do more than wish for the happy ending, you can make it happen.

Similarly, the website of Habitat for Humanity, a charity that depends on volunteers to donate money, material, and time to build houses for "deserving families," features stories of those who have received houses (and of those who have volunteered). As I am writing this, the first of a dozen stories is about Nadya and Ivan Hadziev who live in a remote district of Sofia, Bulgaria's capital, and have three children. Their 10-year-old twin boys, Mihail and Mitko, were born with cerebral palsy. Mitko is less affected, while Mihail moves around only in a wheelchair (Bezgachina 2010). Immediately we begin filling in the story, imagining its possible denouements, and caring about what happens to this family.

A quick look at the websites of United Way, the Make-a-Wish Foundation, the American Red Cross, and other prominent charities seeking contributions reveals the same technique. Indeed, the panhandler approaching me on the street does the same, telling me a tale of misfortune. (I am not equating these things, of course.) And we know the power of these stories, which is why we sometimes respond by shutting our ears, by refusing to listen to the stories. We know that if we hear out the panhandler, even though part of our brain recognizes that he is likely trying to con us, we also know that we could be caught up in his story, and if we were, it would be psychologically difficult to resist.

## Ideological Interests

Ideological interests involve preferences for certain states of the world: for limited government, environmental stewardship, banning abortion, and the like. Although ideological preferences often coincide with self-interest—the wealthy tend to have an ideological preference for lower taxes and fewer public services—some ideological interests have a much more tenuous connection to material well-being.

When self-interest is not the basis for ideological stands, how is it that people come to take them, often quite passionately? One answer lies with the power of ideological narratives.

Consider the ideological interest of members of the "Tea Party." As Theda Skocpol and Vanessa Williamson (2012) document, self-identified members of the Tea Party, the conservative political movement that took off shortly after Barack Obama was sworn into office, have a well-defined ideology. Government is "out of control," freedom is under attack, "freeloaders" are undeserving beneficiaries of government handouts, and immigrants are a threat to America. They have a particular loathing for President Obama, who is viewed as not really one of us and who is an exemplar of "an elite class that loathes the middle class," in the words of one Tea Partier. Their mission, therefore, is to "take America back," to restore the Constitution and the original vision of the Founding Fathers.

Where did these interests come from? To be sure, many of the goals of Tea Partiers are aligned with egoistic interests: lower taxes, for example, are consistent with a party that is wealthier than the average American. But "taking America back," restoring the Constitution, and returning to the Founding Fathers are goals that only make sense in the context of a narrative in which America has been taken from *us* by some *other*. The basis for these interests is a story in which personal freedom is under assault by liberals, socialists, and big government.

In a speech given at a rally in Atlanta, for example, a Tea Party member told the tale:

"For almost a hundred years, Americans have been standing by while our government has been slowly destroying our Constitution, we have watched our liberties and our freedoms erode away, we have stood by while our elected officials let lobbyists and special interest groups influence policy making. America has endured betrayal, lies, dishonor and zero accountability...." (Ridgel 2010)

A video on the website of "Tea Party Patriots" (2010) entitled "We the People (The Revolution)" shows images of protestors at a Washington, D.C., rally holding signs such as "The U.S. Constitution must be defended. If need be I will do so with my LIFE!" and "NO to Big Government" and "I WANT MY COUNTRY BACK!" A musician performs a ballad:

> The Nation that we knew is quickly fading
> Our liberties are slipping every day
> And the devil in disguise has brought damnation with his lies
> That he can give us peace and take the pain away.

[An image of Barack Obama appears at this point.]

> The Founding Fathers wrote the Constitution
> To show us how to keep our people free
> the governmental laws are breaking down our Fathers' walls
> With their darkest plans enslaving you and me. (Girard 2010)

The Tea Party narrative needs little explication. The plot is an unfolding tragedy: In the beginning the Founding Fathers created this nation, and it was good. Now we are on a path towards socialism (hell!). The villains are clear: big government, liberals, elites, and Obama. So, too, the victims: "you and me." If one accepts this narrative and enters the reality it creates, it is hard not to want the story to turn out differently, to have an "interest" in averting tragedy.

Environmental interests in combating climate change, to take another example, can also derive from tragic narrative. That individuals would have such an interest is far from given. First, they need to believe that climate change is happening and that it will have negative consequences, which is not something that can be discerned from personal experience. And even if they have such beliefs, an interest in limiting climate change is not inevitable, since most significant impacts are likely to occur well into the future. Yet even without an egoistic interest in the matter, some environmentalists clearly have quite a passionate concern.

Where, then, might such an interest come from? Most likely from the emotional power of narratives about climate change. Consider, for example, the stories told in *An Inconvenient Truth*, the Academy Award–winning documentary featuring Al Gore's efforts to persuade Americans of the need to act. *An Inconvenient Truth* tells the climate change story as an impending tragedy, with a series of sad sub-narratives about receding glaciers, stranded polar bears, rising seas swamping major cities, and violent storms like Hurricane Katrina devastating cities like New Orleans. Before-and-after photos show the shrinking snow cap of Mount Kilimanjaro; if this continues, Gore laments, "there will be no more snows of Kilimanjaro." Perhaps the most poignant image is that of Earth viewed as a tiny planet from deep space. Gore narrates:

> Everything that has ever happened in all of human history has happened on that pixil. All the triumphs and tragedies. All the wars. All the famines....It's our only home. And that is what is at stake. Our ability to live on Planet Earth. To have a future as a civilization. (Guggenheim 2006)

In Gore's telling, we are all cast as victims, at stake is the fate of the Earth, of civilization, of humanity.

What evidence is there that the movie had an impact? For one thing, the movie was enormously popular, a box office hit. And those who viewed the film said it affected their beliefs. In a 47-country Internet survey conducted by The Nielsen Company and Oxford University in July 2007, 66 percent of viewers who claimed to have seen *An Inconvenient Truth* said the film had "changed their mind" about global warming, and 89 percent said watching the movie made them more aware of the problem. Three out of four (74 percent) viewers said they changed some of their habits as a result of seeing the film (Nielsen 2007).

Of course, ideological interests related to climate change are not confined to supporters of taking action to combat it. Opponents have constructed climate change as a "fraud" and a "hoax," part of a conspiracy by United Nations scientists and liberal elites to empower government and limit personal freedom. These narratives, propagated on Fox News and other conservative media outlets, appear to have had a significant impact in creating an interest in opposing action on climate change among segments of the American public (Krosnick 2010; Mayer, 2012; Feldman, Malbach, Roser-Renouf and Leiserowitz 2012).

Fictional narratives can be as powerful as non-fiction in establishing ideological interests. Engrossed by a powerful fictional narrative, we accept its premises, and its meaning. Historians agree that Harriet Beecher Stowe's *Uncle Tom's Cabin*, the most widely read American book of the 19th century, was enormously influential in shaping public opposition to slavery. (Lincoln is reported to have said upon meeting her: "So this is the little lady who started this great war.") The meaning of Stowe's narrative, on one level a story about one slave's suffering and his owner's villainy, is at a deeper level about the cruelty and injustice of slavery itself. Engrossed in the compelling narrative, it was hard not to view slavery in a different light (Goldner 2001; Gerrig 1993).

## Patriotic Interests

A patriotic interest involves concern with the fate of one's community. Patriotism and altruism are clearly related, but patriotism is less an interest in others' welfare, even if others are part of one's group, than an interest in the welfare of the group itself. Patriotism may also have an element of egoistic interest; one could reason that if my country, tribe, or team does well, so will I. But love of country can be quite selfless; indeed, some people are willing to die for it.

Whatever other sources there may be for patriotism, engrossment in a narrative in which one's country (or tribe, clan, school or other such community) is the sympathetic protagonist and whose fortunes are the primary driver of the plot is the basis for many patriotic sentiments. Narratives about us—whether the *us* is our country, our clan, or our school—create interests in the fate of the collective. When I root for the United States in the Olympics, I do so not because I think winning the Olympics will be good for Americans, but because I want America to do well in the unfolding drama that is the Olympics.

Patriotic narratives often cast the nation as the virtuous hero doing battle with evil others. Sometimes the stories are in the context of actual battle: the story of the Boston Tea Party in the American Revolution, the Confederate narrative of the Old South defending its honor and way of life against the Yankee invasion, the "Remember the Maine" story of Spanish perfidy against America, and Cold War narratives of America under assault from communism within and without. All served to evoke anger and patriotic fervor. Gripped by such stories, it is impossible not to desire to defend the homeland and to avenge the treachery of our enemies.[4]

Consider the story told by President Bush in the immediate aftermath of 9/11. As noted earlier, in his telling, the attacks that leveled the World Trade Center Towers and damaged the Pentagon were an act of war against America, and not, as was logically possible, a criminal action by a band of fanatical extremists. So framed as an episode in the American story, in which America was clearly the victim and "terror" the villain, the response of war became the patriotic interest, as those who counseled restraint quickly realized. As Brands (2008) has documented, once we were a "nation at war," as the scroll at the bottom of the television news feeds trumpeted, opposition to war was considered close to unpatriotic.

Not all patriotic narratives are about conflict with others. Some are progress stories, in which the community is born, comes of age, and becomes better, freer, stronger, and the like, usually because of its virtue. Others are stories of decline, in which internal enemies are sapping its strength, the country has lost its way, the virtues that made it strong are in decline, and so on. In the grip of these stories, one roots for continued triumph or hopes for restoration.

## A Note on Values

Interests are often distinguished from values, although the line dividing them is not sharp. Values are broad general preferences for behavior and outcomes that have an intrinsically moral content. They are such things as integrity, loyalty, fairness, generosity, justice, and freedom.

Narrative is central both to establishing our core values and to framing issues in terms of those values. As we explored in Chapter 4, stories have a moral as well as a causal logic. Those who seek to teach or invoke morality use stories. Parents, teachers, and preachers tell stories to their children, their students, and their congregations, stories in which virtue is rewarded and vice punished. As we will explore further in the next chapter, society uses narrative to convey its core values. In the Christian Bible, when Jesus seeks to teach that morality requires compassion to strangers he tells a story, the parable of the Good Samaritan.

> A Jewish man was travelling on a trip from Jerusalem to Jericho, and he was attacked by bandits. They stripped him of his clothes, beat him up, and left him half dead beside the road. By chance a priest came along. But when he saw the man lying there, he crossed to the other side of the road and passed him by. A Levite walked over and looked at him lying there, but he also passed by on the other side. Then a despised Samaritan came along, and when he saw the man, he felt compassion for him. Going over to him, the Samaritan soothed his wounds with olive oil and wine and bandaged them. Then he put the man on his own donkey and took him to an inn, where he took care of him. The next day he handed the innkeeper two silver coins, telling him, "Take care of this man. If his bill runs higher than this, I'll pay you the next time I'm here." "Now which of these three would you say was a neighbor to the man who was attacked by bandits?" Jesus asked. The man replied, "The one who showed him mercy." Then Jesus said, "Yes, now go and do the same." (Luke 10:30-7)

In this story, Jesus is teaching what it means to be moral through a story in which the Samaritan does the right thing.

So, too, the stories told about Jesus in the Bible—of the loaves and the fishes, the money changers in the Temple, the last supper, and the crucifixion—the stories of the Jewish Torah—of Abraham and Isaac and David and Solomon—the stories of Mohammed and of Buddha and of gods and humans in so many other religions; and indeed all secular stories in which the bad guys lose and the good guys win, in which virtue is rewarded and vice punished: all create a desire to do the right thing. They are intended to teach us what is moral, to make us fit for life in society.

## IDENTIFICATION AND IDENTITY

In the previous chapter I discussed how we use self-narrative to establish our identity. Missing in that discussion was an acknowledgment of how narratives of others, those contained in books, movies, myths, and tales told to us at bedtime, provide templates for our self-story, provide the possible plots and character types and meanings from which we construct our own life story. And for that reason, stories not only persuade, not only moralize, but also, sometimes, change our identity, or, to be more precise, enable us to imagine a different life narrative and to see "ourselves as another" (Ricoeur 1995).

The impact of narrative on identity depends on identification with characters in the stories that engross us. When we enter a story, we become, for a time, the swashbuckling Robin outwitting the sheriff, the mysterious Batman doing battle with villains, the downtrodden Cinderella rescued by the prince, the brave Dorothy defeating the wicked witch, or, in the realm of public life, Bobby or Martin or Mandela. The psychologist Robert Coles (1989) describes Phil, a young man who found himself captivated by *Catcher in the Rye* (an experience many in my generation have had). Phil strongly identified with Holden Caulfield, the alienated protagonist of Salinger's classic. Soon, Phil was talking about "what it means to be honest and decent in a world full of 'phoniness.'" As Coles observes, "Holden's voice (Salinger's) had become Phil's and uncannily, Holden's dreams of escape, of rescue (to save not only himself but others), had become Phil's. The novel had, as he put it, 'got' to him" (Coles 1989, 38). Now, Phil saw "phoniness" everywhere. Through narrative identification, he had assumed the perspective, the stance, the attitude of another, and that identification enabled "an emerging angle of vision in himself..." (Coles 1989, 39).

Stories can take us out of ourselves and let us try on different roles, and at the same time hold up our own world to ourselves so that we see ourselves fresh, sometimes in painful clarity. Through imagining ourselves as another, we recast ourselves, reinterpreting our story to date or envisioning the story yet to come. When we return from our role-plays, we have new possibilities for seeing ourselves as challenging the sheriffs of our day, ridding our Gothams of bad guys, waiting for the prince with our glass slipper, seeing through the pretense of wizards, or any of the infinite variations, heroic or not, that sympathetic characters can take. For Camus, identifying with Sisyphus means seeing oneself as condemned forever to push the stone up the hill, at once terrifying and absurd, yet also, perhaps a path towards happiness: "The struggle itself toward the heights is enough to fill a man's heart. One must imagine Sisyphus happy" (Camus 1955, 91).

For example, many of our students at Duke find the story of Paul Farmer inspiring. Farmer (a Duke alumnus) is a physician whose life work has been to secure healthcare for many of the world's poor. His life story is the subject of Tracy Kidder's *Mountains Beyond Mountains: The Quest of Doctor Paul Farmer, The Man Who Would Cure the World* (Kidder 2003). It is difficult, when reading Farmer's life story, not to be inspired, not to want to be like him. For most, the identification will be short-lived, but for a few, the inspiration will be transformative.

## ACTING THE PART: THE DRAMATIC IMPERATIVE

It is one thing to imagine; it is another to act. As I explored in the last chapter, human behavior is often as much a matter of enactment as of choice or habit. We act in ways that are intelligible, that are meaningful, in the sense that they can be explained in the context of a story we tell ourselves. When we are drawn into a story told by others, we may come to see ourselves as characters in the unfolding drama and find that we are compelled to act, compelled to do the moral thing, compelled to do what our identity demands of us, compelled by the dramatic imperative of the narrative.

In Tolkien's epic *Lord of the Rings*, Frodo, exhausted and discouraged, despairs of succeeding as they struggle ever closer to Mordor. His companion Sam urges him on.

> "And we shouldn't be here at all, if we'd known more about it before we started. But I suppose it's often that way. The brave things in the old tales and songs, Mr. Frodo: adventures, as I used to call them. I used to think that they were things the wonderful folk of the stories went out and looked for, because they wanted

them, because they were exciting and life was a bit dull, a kind of a sport, as you might say.

But that's not the way of it with the tales that really mattered, or the ones that stay in the mind. Folk seem to have been just landed in them, usually—their paths were laid that way, as you put it. But I expect they had lots of chances, like us, of turning back, only they didn't. And if they had, we shouldn't know, because they'd have been forgotten." (Tolkien 1954, 362)

And so they carry on, compelled to see the story through.

There is wisdom in this fictional work, but such things do not only happen in fiction. In 2005, Charlie Weis, then the new football coach at Notre Dame, perhaps the most storied football program in the country, met Montana Mazurkiewicz, a 10-year-old Notre Dame fan who was dying of cancer, and asked whether there was anything he could do for the boy. Montana asked if he could call the first play of the next football game. Weis promised to do it. Montana died the day before the game.

In the locker room on game day, Weis told the story to his team to make the point that they "represented a lot of people they didn't even know they were representing" (Condotta 2005). And the first play would be a pass—Montana's wish. According to an eyewitness, you could have heard a pin drop in the locker room. As it happened, however, Notre Dame fumbled the opening kickoff and only barely managed to recover the ball on its own one-yard line.

Normally, backed up against the goal line, teams call a running play to minimize the risk of a safety. As the boy's mother later said, "I thought, 'There's no way he's going to be able to make that pass. Not from where they're at. He's going to get sacked and Washington's [the opponent] going to get two points.'" And as Weis later said, his quarterback asked "What are we going to do?" Weis said "We have no choice. We're throwing to the right" (Associated Press 2009). The Notre Dame quarterback threw to his tight end, who leapt over a defender to make an improbable catch at the 14-yard line.

Why did Coach Weis call for a pass play on his own 1-yard line? In terms of football strategy, the play was unintelligible. But he had to keep his promise. In the context of the drama in which Weis, his team, and the boy's family were cast, Weis's action was what the story required.

So, too, in social and political life, we can be called to act by the stories that engross us, as the next two chapters will explore. Caught up in story, pulled up onto the stage, we find that we must rescue the victim, must fight for justice, must sacrifice for the cause, because our identity is at stake, because those acts are what the plot demands of our character. That is why those who call us to action—charities, advocates, teachers, coaches, leaders of all types—strive to engross us in a story in which we are compelled to act by the dramatic imperative of the narrative.

# PART THREE

# *Narrative and Collective Action*

## CHAPTER 6

# Constructing the Collective Good

*There is no way to give us an understanding of any society, including our own, except through
the stock of stories which constitute its initial dramatic resources.*
Alisdair MacIntyre (1981, 216)

*Every people gets the politics it imagines*
Clifford Geertz (1973, 313)

Before a community can engage in collective action, its members must share an interest in some end: protecting civil rights, ending abortion, preventing climate change, combatting terrorism, banning landmines, resisting globalization, promoting democracy, or some other common concern. That an individual would have such interests is far from inevitable; that a group share them is even more problematic. Interests of these kinds do not inevitably arise out of circumstance and primal concerns for security, power or wealth. Rather, they must be constructed through some mechanism. Indeed, they must be *commonly* constructed, so that individual interests align to form a shared interest in a collective good.

In the last chapter, we saw how narratives can alter individual beliefs and construct interests. But narratives are not only transporting, they are also *transportable*. We *share* stories. Because narratives can be held simultaneously in many minds, they make it possible for individuals to "transcend their different private worlds" (Ragnar Rommetviet, quoted in Wertsch 1998, 112) and "appropriate to assign to groups as well as to individuals terms such as 'think,' 'attend' and 'remember'"(Wertsch 1998, 111). And just as narratives in mind can construct interests, shared narratives held in many minds can create common interests.

In this chapter I explore how and under what circumstances narratives have this power. I argue that several factors contribute to the efficacy of narratives, among them alignment with material self-interest and frequency of exposure. I stress, however, that the power of particular narratives also depends on their resonance with the stories a community already holds in mind, particularly with the public narratives—religious, historical, ideological and popular—that are at the core of a community's culture.

I begin, therefore, with a description of the landscape of public narratives and their role in creating a community's identity, worldview, and ethos. The canon of a community's public narratives can also be thought of as constituting a core element of its *collective memory*. The literature on collective memory derives from the work of the French scholar Maurice Halbwachs on the social basis of memory. For Halbwachs, "it is in society that people normally acquire their memories. It is also in society that they recall, recognize, and localize their memories" (Halbwachs and Coser 1992, 38). Although collective memory is held in the minds of individuals, those memories are established and reinforced through the shared rituals of society. Just as individual memory is central to individual cognition, affect, and identity, collective memory plays an important role in aligning individual minds into common consciousness, shared passion, and collective identity.

In foregrounding the narrative dimensions of collective memory and their functions, I am not arguing for cultural determinism any more than I am arguing for material determinism. Rather, I am taking a middle position with respect to the relative importance of cultural factors and material interests, with respect to the balance between socialization and individual agency, and with respect to whether collective memory is relatively stable over time or is constantly recreated to suit the needs of the present. My orientation draws particularly on the work of the Russian scholars Lev Vygotsky and Mikhail Bahktin, especially as interpreted in the work of American anthropologist James Wertsch, whose concept of "mediated action" provides a way of thinking of cultural texts as tools that enable but do not determine thought and action, and who conceives of collective memory as similarly mediated by the text of culture. My argument is that public narratives at once establish a community's basic orientations—its worldview and its ethos—and serve as what MacIntyre (1997) has called an "initial cultural stock" from which new stories may draw, either by directly referencing them or by appealing to the basic understandings of who *we* are, what *we* believe, and what *we* value that they construct.

I then turn to a discussion of how political actors use narrative to construct shared interests in collective goods. As I discussed in chapter 2, complex interests involve two elements: an underlying core interest in some outcome and a belief about the implications of some action for that outcome. For shared egoistic interests, in security for example, narrative may only be needed to construct beliefs about what course of action serves that fundamental interest. But for non-egoistic interests, in reducing current carbon emissions to benefit future generations, for example, narrative may also be crucial for constructing the core interest itself, in this case environmental protection. To assert that narrative *can* construct such interests, however, does not predict when it will. For that reason I explore the question of what factors affect when a story will be taken up by a community, acknowledging that the efficacy of a story depends in part on alignment with material interests and in part on who has access to the megaphone, but also arguing that the power of the story depends on the skill of the storyteller in telling a story that resonates with the stories a community already has in mind, with the narratives of culture.

## THE NARRATIVE LANDSCAPE OF CULTURE

To be in a culture is to share a canon of public narratives—religious, historical, ideological, and popular—that together constitute a society's mythology, in the sense that myths are "the stories that tell a society what is important for it to know, whether about its gods, its history, its laws, or its class structure" (Frye 1982, 33).[1] The canon of available public narratives is a central element of a community's collective memory. As such, it helps define common identity, determining who "we" are (and who is "other") and what kind of people we are, and helps establish common beliefs about how the world works and what a community views as proper, just, and moral.

Religion has historically been a core element of culture in most societies. And at the heart of every religion are narratives: creation myths, stories of gods and humans, stories that deal with the vagaries of fate and the possibilities for agency, stories that define what is right and what is wrong. As Hauerwas has said, "There is no more fundamental way to talk of God than in a story" (Hauerwas 1983, quoted in Jackson 1995, 9). Judeo-Christian narratives have long been a central element of Western culture, and, therefore, particularly important elements of the American cultural landscape. Exodus—the escape from slavery in the symbolic hell of Egypt and the long journey to the Promised Land—and the Christ story—the birth, death and resurrection of Jesus—are clearly the most important. Many other Biblical stories are also deeply ingrained: Adam and Eve, Noah and the Ark, David and Goliath, and the Good Samaritan, to name just a few.

A community typically also has a set of widely shared historical narratives, including accounts of how it began, how it arrived where it is today, and where it might be going. This might be called its *folk history*, the story a community tells itself about its past.[2] The predominant folk history of the United States illustrates the point. Wertsch reports on experiments in which high school students asked to produce accounts of American history converge around a "quest-for-freedom narrative" (Wertsch 1998, 88). As with autobiographical memory, the salient incidents are those that figure most prominently in the larger narrative sweep: the colonization by Europeans seeking religious freedom, the Revolutionary War cast as a war for the colonies' freedom, the Civil War as the great test of freedom, the World Wars in which the United States saves the world from tyranny, the civil rights movement as making good on the promise of freedom for all Americans, and the Cold War as a triumph of American economic and political freedom over communism.[3] Events that do not fit the larger narrative are either reframed as bumps in the road or simply left out altogether. The fate of Native Americans and the failure of the Vietnam War, for example, have relatively low salience. A strong element of "American exceptionalism" also permeates America's folk history, a theme that nests the historical within the religious. In this telling, not only is America the great champion of freedom, but also Americans are the chosen people, called to be, as John Winthrop put it at the beginning, a "city upon a hill." (Winthrop 1994).

Ideological communities share ideological narratives—stories about politics, society and public policy. These narratives convey basic orientations towards such matters as the proper roles for governments and markets, the balance between individual freedom and social obligation, or particular stances on such issues as abortion, gun ownership, and environmental protection. Contemporary American conservatives, for example, share a political ideology in which the meta-narrative is essentially a "fall" story. In the beginning, set in some vaguely located golden past, America was strong, its people self-reliant, its government limited, its markets strong and productive, and its families intact and moral. Liberals (the villains) brought America down by erecting a welfare state ("big government"), which spawned dependency, created a permissive environment in which crime and deviancy flourished, overtaxed and over-regulated the market, and weakened the military and law enforcement.[4] In contrast, at the heart of American liberalism is a progress narrative. From the Emancipation Proclamation and the end of slavery, to the suffragettes and women's right to vote, to the civil rights movement and its triumph over Jim Crow, to the effort to extend equal rights to gay Americans, the story is a journey towards freedom and equality.

Communities also share popular myths. At different points in American history, certain tales have been particularly prominent. One genre has concerned our relationship to nature. In colonial America, captivity narratives enjoyed enormous popularity. In these tales, in which typically a European was captured by the "savage" Native Americans and then rescued, nature (and the native people who exemplified it) were depicted as forces to be feared, controlled, and subdued. Later, the Daniel Boone legend offered an alternative vision of nature. The Boone stories involve a series of immersions into the wilderness, which is no longer a symbolic hell but a reflection of the divine order (Slotkin 1973). Civilization and its corruptions became the villains; nature the victim. Boone served as an archetype for many American fictional heroes that followed, from Cooper's Natty Bumpo to the typical hero of the American Western: a solitary, tough, and incorruptible figure. For Robert Jewett and John Lawrence, this is the American "monomyth":

> A community in a harmonious paradise is threatened by evil; normal institutions fail to contend with this threat; a selfless superhero emerges to renounce temptations and carry out the redemptive task; aided by fate, his decisive victory restores the community to it paradisiacal condition; the superhero then recedes into obscurity. (Jewett and Lawrence 2002, 6)

By all-too-briefly surveying the landscape of American public narratives, my point is not to provide anything approaching a comprehensive picture. Rather, it is to demonstrate the range of shared narratives that members of a community will hold in mind. Too be clear, too, I am not arguing that every member of a community will subscribe to every narrative. Even within communities, there may be contests among competing narratives. And in the contemporary world, we are all members of many communities, religious, political, ideological, and other. Nonetheless, within each of these communities there are shared cultural spaces defined in part by these kinds of public narratives.

## COLLECTIVE IDENTITY, SHARED WORLDVIEW, AND COMMON ETHOS

What work, then, are these public narratives doing? In part, they serve for communities many of the same functions that private narratives serve for individuals. They help to define who *we* are, what *we* believe, and what *we* value. As Malinowski (1926) said about myth, public narrative "expresses, enhances and codifies belief; it vouches for the efficacy of ritual and contains practical rules for the guidance of man. Myth is then a vital ingredient of human civilization; it is not an idle tale but a hard-worked active force" (quoted in Miller 1994, 158). So, too, is myth in contemporary society, although it is always harder to recognize one's own myths as such.

## Collective Identity

Shared narratives are not just a consequence of being in community, they also help to constitute the community in the first instance. As individual identity is constituted by autobiographical narrative, so is community identity by its autobiography, by its history. As Carr puts it, "[a] community... exists by virtue of a story which is articulated and accepted, which typically concerns the group's origins and its destiny, and which interprets what is happening now in the light of these two temporal poles" (Carr 1997, 20). By sharing a story about "us," a people comes to see itself as a whole, comes to see the community as an actor in a history.[5]

The way in which narrative can delimit who is included in the "we" (and who is not) is nicely illustrated by Wills' (1992) exploration of Lincoln's Gettysburg Address. After the carnage at Gettysburg and the pivotal Union victory over Robert E. Lee's Army of the Confederacy, nothing would have been more natural than to honor the dead Union soldiers as heroes in a battle between the "us" of the North and the "them" of the South. Yet Lincoln's genius was that he rejected such a formulation in favor of a story in which the central character was the nation as a whole, and the villain was the war itself. His short speech told the nation's story. "Fourscore and seven years ago" he began, "our forefathers brought forth... a new nation, conceived in liberty and dedicated to the proposition that all men are created equal." The war was the pivotal moment in the national story, "testing whether that nation, or any nation so conceived and so dedicated, can long endure." Thus framed, tragedy would be to fail the test, triumph "that government of the people, by the people, for the people, shall not perish from the earth." Whatever its impact in the moment, the Gettysburg Address has become a nearly sacred document in America's historical imagination, and part of the historical canon to which contemporary leaders commonly refer when they seek to remind Americans of their common identity (Wills 1992).[6]

Beyond defining "we," a community's narratives also establish what kind of character "we" are. In America's self-story, for example, the United States is cast as the chosen nation, the freest, most democratic, most vigorous and virtuous on earth. From John Winthrop's description of America as a "City on a Hill," America has seen itself as exceptional, a beacon of hope to the world, the champion of liberty, the land of opportunity, in which those who work hard and live virtuously can share in the "American Dream." American exceptionalism echoes Biblical notions of the chosen people, in which God is seen playing a hand in America's expansion and rise to power, as in narratives of America's "manifest destiny."

Myths that establish core national identities are certainly not unique to the American experience. The Masada myth is central to the identity of contemporary Israelis, for example (Ben-Yehuda 1995). The story is of heroic resistance by a "small group of Jewish warriers [who] fought to the bitter end against overwhelming odds and a *much* larger Roman army" (Ben-Yehuda 1995, 10). In the words of Moshe Dayan, the Masada myth says that Israelis are the people who "fight to the death rather than surrender; prefer death to bondage and loss of freedom" (quoted in Ben-Yehuda 1995, 14). Similarly, in contemporary France, the story of the Nazi atrocities in the village of Oradour has become a central part of the French national memory of World War II. In June 1944, Nazi soldiers entered the village, sealed the town entrances, separated the men from women and children, and systematically massacred the entire population. As Sarah Farmer (1999) has documented, the story as remembered is one in which all resisted and none collaborated. Farmer argues that the story serves to help the French see themselves as resisters and victims of the Nazis, and not as passive and complicit.

Events that conflict with a community's identity tend not to be included in its historical narrative. For example, the dominant historical narrative of white Atlanta managed to completely suppress its memory of the Atlanta Race Riot of 1906, in which a startling fraction of adult white males went on a two-day rampage against Atlanta's black neighborhoods and business district, and in which perhaps as many as 100 African Americans died (Dittmer 1977). Yet within a couple days after the uprising, no further mention of the riots found their way into the white newspapers, and there was, until the 1970s, no mention in the official histories of Atlanta. How could an event of such magnitude, arguably the most important between Sherman's burning of Atlanta and the Olympic games of 1996, be "forgotten"? The answer is that the story did not fit with its identity as the progressive city of the "New South" after the Civil War, whose mayor declared it a "city too busy to hate" during the turmoil of the civil rights movement. Of course, memories of the riot lived on in the African American community, which saw Atlanta in a very different light.

## Worldviews and Ethos

Public narratives also help to establish a community's basic beliefs and values, its *worldview* and its *ethos*. A worldview can be thought of as the shared cognitive schemata of society: general institutionalized knowledge that establishes categories and causal patterns. An ethos can be thought of as the shared normative schemata of society: general orientations and values that describe the proper order of things and that define the rules and obligations of moral behavior.[7] Both are shaped by shared religious, historical, ideological, and popular narratives.

Religious narratives obviously convey moral messages. But in addition to their normative content, they also carry with them beliefs about the way the world works and why things are as they are. In Clifford Geertz's words, religion allows for "the formulation, by means of symbols, of an image of such a genuine order of the world which will account for, and even celebrate, the perceived ambiguities, puzzles, and paradoxes in human experience" (Geertz 1973, 108). For example, as Michael Walzer (1985) has explored, Exodus provides a perspective about the role of divinely inspired leadership in human affairs, about the meaning of hardships in life, and about the prospects for ultimate rewards. The Exodus narrative has been particularly important in shaping the worldview of the African American community, as the historian Taylor Branch (1989) has powerfully documented. It has provided a way of making sense of the tribulations of slavery and Jim Crow, and of seeing the civil rights movement as a journey out of Egypt. King's acute awareness of that narrative tradition and his skill as a preacher in drawing upon it were the source of his extraordinary rhetorical power, as Richard Lischer (1995) has shown.

Historical narratives establish a community's worldview and ethos. For example, in the American story, America's emergence in the 20th Century as the pre-eminent global power is framed not as an accident of geography and history (the beneficiary of the devastation of other powers by World War II), but rather as the consequence of our virtue. Similarly, in an earlier era, America's westward expansion was viewed as a matter of "manifest destiny," (Merk and Merk, 27) a term coined in 1845 that summarized a narrative in which, in Andrew Jackson's words, annexation was about "extending the area of freedom," (Correspondence of Andrew Jackson, ed. John Spencer Bassett, quoted in Wilson 1967, 623).

Historical tales also teach particular "lessons of history" and serve as touchstones for those who use narrative to construct the meaning of contemporary events. The story of Chamberlain's 1938 capitulation in Munich to Hitler's annexation of the Sudetenland, often invoked in US politics, is a parable about the dangers of appeasement, an available trope for making sense of subsequent events. As Yuen Foong Khong (1992) has documented, the Munich fable was very much in the minds of Lyndon Johnson and his circle of advisors as they made the fateful decisions in 1965 that committed the United States to deep engagement in Vietnam. In Johnson's words,

> a great many people started by compromising and trying to mediate the situation. And Chamberlin [sic] came back and he thought he had obtained peace in our time, but it remained for Churchill—who had warned all these years of the dangers...to rise to the occasion....
>
> I frequently referred to the fact that Churchill standing alone, after the Battle of Britain and after France had fallen, and after it looked like fascism was in the ascendency—that Churchill almost by himself had provided the courage and the resistance that stopped Hitler. (Khong 1992, 176)

Johnson desperately sought to avoid being Chamberlain, and sought, in vain, for a Vietnamese Churchill, who would stop the dominos from falling as they had in Europe after Munich. Of course, academic historians have a much more nuanced view of Chamberlain and his role that is certainly nothing like the caricature of the popular historical narrative (McDonough 2002).

Similarly, after the Vietnam War, the story of "Vietnam" became a countervailing parable (although somewhat more contested than that of "Munich"), a cautionary tale about the potential "quagmire" of foreign intervention.[8] Marvin Kalb and Deborah Kalb (2011) document how the specter of Vietnam, a story in which a well-meaning America finds itself trapped in an endless war with no prospect of clear victory, shaped the views of foreign policy makers in the years after the war. When Yugoslavia came apart at the end of George H. W. Bush's administration, for example, and evidence of Serbian atrocities against Bosnian Muslims mounted, the legacy of Vietnam weighed heavily on Bush and his advisors. As Hal Brands notes, "[b]y late 1992, the lessons of Vietnam had become omnipresent in Bush's statements on Bosnia and other areas rife with ethnic strife" (Brands 2008, 91). The same framing limited President Clinton's initial response in Bosnia, as it would also shape his decision to withdraw from Somalia and his hesitancy to commit any ground forces in Kosovo in 1999. Not surprisingly, Bush and Clinton's caution evoked the appeasement narrative from those favoring intervention, with Serbian behavior characterized as "genocide." The editors of *The New Republic* published a book titled *The Black Book of Bosnia: The Consequences of Appeasement*, the reference being to the "Black Book" of Jewish names kept by the Nazis (Mousavizadeh 1996). The discourse over what to do in Bosnia became essentially a contest of two competing narratives, one in which Bosnia was another Vietnam, the other in which inaction was another Munich (Hansen 2006). [9]

It is useful to note that the familiarity of the Munich and Vietnam parables is such that each can be invoked without actually retelling the story. If might seem, therefore, that both might be better classified as symbols or metaphors than as narratives. Yet, because we know the moral of the story, the *fabula*, we don't need to actually tell a tale with beginning, middle, and end in order to invoke it. If pushed to explain our meaning, we know the narrative that produced the moral and can reconstruct the story that "must have been."

Ideological narratives convey the beliefs and attitudes of political communities. Individuals generally are poorly informed about policy and politics, as Downs' (1957) theory of "rational ignorance" would predict. Nevertheless, political communities tend to have reasonably coherent beliefs and values that are "among several correlated dimensions of a master concept, ideology" (Zaller 1992, 26). The puzzle is how communities reach such coherence. A clue is to recognize that ideology is at its heart a form of political mythology, a collection of narratives that together establish shared positive and normative schema about such matters as the proper role of government, the virtues (or evils) of free markets, and the use of force in international affairs (Flood 1996; Bottici 2007). Classic Marxism, to take a clear case, involves an epic contest between capital and labor, a tragic tale of exploitation that can only be redeemed through revolution.

Some ideological narratives may be shared by an entire national community. In the United States, many of our stories convey suspicion of government and politicians (the original Boston Tea Party, for example), while others transmit our belief in the American Dream of rising from poverty to wealth through personal virtue. Other ideological narratives are shared within narrower political communities of like-minded citizens—Republicans and Democrats, for example—or even more narrowly, contemporary Tea Party members and environmental activists. These communities will tell different stories, and differ, therefore, in their perspective on such matters as the roles of governments and markets, and the international order and America's place in it; their beliefs about such policy questions as the causes of poverty (circumstance or volition), climate change (man or nature), and the AIDS pandemic (disease or behavior); and their value judgments about such issues as abortion, civil liberties, and affirmative action. The division here between historical and ideological narratives is somewhat artificial, of course. Historical narratives are almost inevitably ideological, and ideological narratives are often framed as history.

## SOCIALIZATION, AGENCY, AND THE POLITICS
## OF PUBLIC NARRATIVE

The discussion of the relationship of cultural texts to community identity, worldviews, and ethos has so far elided two issues. The first concerns the mechanism through which those texts are transmitted from society to the individual, with its implications for the relative importance of socialization on the one hand and the possibility of individual agency on the other. The second concerns the stability of public narratives, particular the extent to which they are either relatively timeless and stable or largely reinvented to reflect present circumstances, a debate central to the literature on collective memory. I will take a middle position on both issues: we are neither fully culturally determined nor fully autonomous, and the texts of our culture are neither static inheritances nor completely malleable.

Humans are social animals, made whole through the acquisition of social knowledge, beginning with language itself, and including more complex symbolic structures such as narrative. We are *socialized*. As Mead put it about the human being, "The very speech he uses, the very mechanics of thought which is given, are social products. His own self is attained only though his taking on the attitudes of the social group to which he belongs. He must be socialized to become himself" (Mead 1934, 18).

Not surprisingly, sociologists and cultural anthropologists have tended to emphasize the role of social processes and structures in shaping individual cognition, even when they disagree sharply on the genesis and nature of those structures. For Durkheim and other functionalists, the purpose of culture was to maintain the institutions of society, enable the resolution of conflict, and socialize individual behavior in ways that serve society. Marx shared this functionalist view of culture, arguing that "[i]t is not the consciousness of men which determines their existence, but on the contrary it is their social existence which determines their consciousness," but saw its purpose, the exploitation of the working class, as less benign (quoted in Burke and Gusfield 1989, 4). A stress on culture as reflection of power has also been at the core of critical studies, which seeks to "deconstruct" the rhetoric that masks the underlying power realities that disadvantage the poor, women, and minorities. As Michel Foucault put it, his project "has been to create a history of the different modes by which, in our culture, human beings are made subjects" (Foucault 1982, 777). For Edward Said, "ideas, cultures, and histories cannot seriously be understood or studied without their force, or more precisely their configuration of power, also being understood" (Said 1979, 5).

In contrast to both the functionalists and critical theorists, symbolic interactionists have had a view of culture as more autonomous and have been more focused on the role of culture in enabling human meaning making. For Geertz, for example, culture is an "historically transmitted pattern of meanings embodied in symbols" (Geertz 1973, 89). Going back to Mead, Geertz and others have stressed the impact of socially constructed symbolic systems not only on what we think but also on how we think. For Mead, the "mind develops and has being only in and by virtue of the social process and activity, which it hence presupposes, and that in no other way can it develop and have its being" (Mead 1934, 243).

The process through which culture is transmitted from society to individual is often left unspecified by those who see culture as determinative; cultural beliefs and norms are said to be "transmitted," "absorbed," and "learned" without much regard to the mechanisms through which this happens. Vygotsky's work is an important exception, however. On the one hand, Vygotsky argued that mental functioning represented an internalization of social interaction: "[I]n their own private sphere, human beings retain the function of social interaction" (quoted in Wertsch 1991, 27). In his studies of childhood development, he explored how children, working with an adult, learn by doing, at first interacting by speaking, for example, and then internalizing speech as a way of thinking. In this way culture enters the mind, including, importantly narrative. On the other hand, Vygotsky insisted that the internalization of culture did not preclude agency. Indeed, it provided the tools for agency, for creative thought and action.

Building on Vygosky, Wertsch argues that we "live in the middle," between cultural forces and individual agency (Wertsch 1998, 141). Wertsch stresses the role of narrative in mediating between society and mind. Storytelling is essential for transmitting culture to the young, for socialization. But the same narrative capacity that allows for the transmission of culture to mind provides the tools for agency and resistance. We are not simply listeners; we are all storytellers, all authors. Our narrativity enables us not only to see how things are, but also, and importantly, to imagine other circumstances. If a human is, as Geertz has said, a creature "suspended in webs of significance he himself has spun" (1973, 5), we are still vigorously spinning.

There remains the issue of the status of the cultural texts themselves, how they are generated, whether they are static or dynamic, and, if dynamic, what determines their content. Here the debate in the collective memory literature is helpful. Most of the literature has a "presentist" orientation, arguing that our collective memory, including both the selection and interpretation of texts, is highly malleable and largely reflects present concerns. Certainly Halbwachs leaned in this direction. As Lewis Coser puts it, "For Halbwachs, the past is a social construction mainly, if not wholly, shaped by the concerns of the present" (Coser 1992, 25). Although they differ in others ways, functionalists in the tradition of Halbwachs, as well as neo-Marxists, are in the first camp, arguing that history is constantly reinvented to serve the interests of society or of the powerful within it. In the other camp, some in cultural studies tend to treat culture as a timeless and independent institution. In some of his writings, Geertz, for example, seems to come close to this position.

As Barry Schwartz has argued, neither extreme stance is satisfactory for understanding collective memory, or what I am calling *folk history*. In two studies, one on the treatment of George Washington and the other of Abraham Lincoln, Schwartz demonstrates that while each figure's story was told differently at different moments in American history—in accounts that clearly reflected the exigencies of the present—there were also elements of continuity in the characterization of both figures and of their meaning (Schwartz 1991; Schwartz 2000). He argues for a middle position. "In most cases, as in the contemplation of Washington, we find the past to be neither totally precarious nor immutable, but a stable image upon which new elements are intermittently superimposed. The past, then, is a familiar rather than a foreign country; its people different, but not strangers to the present" (Schwartz 2000, 303). Consistent with Schwartz, Wertsch treats collective memory as a form of mediated action. On the one hand, the shared texts of culture, what I have called *public narratives*, have a certain stability that arises from the repeated rehearsals they enjoy as part of social life, but on the other, they are sufficiently open-ended as to allow for new interpretations and new uses (Wertsch 2002).

Wertsch's middle stance avoids the danger that by focusing on the role of culture we squeeze out the possibility of agency. As Ortner notes about cultural studies, "the theoretical position generally taken as the more radical is that which excludes an interest in the 'meanings'—the desires and intentions, the beliefs and values—of the very subjects on whose behalf the workings of power are exposed" (Ortner 1999a, 158). And once we accept both the power of narrative and the possibility of agency, we open a space for a politics of narrative. If narrative is as much a tool as it is a text, a tool available to those who would persuade a community of its interests, it matters what stories are told. Stories are always told by someone to someone for some purpose. Although the narratives of culture may provide an initial cultural stock, storytellers have wide latitude both in selecting which to reference and in interpreting them, and therefore in constructing new stories with new meanings. And their audiences retain a measure of autonomy in how they respond to stories, including the ability to resist their messages. Jill Lepore, writing about the uses of the history of the American Revolution by contemporary Tea Partiers, puts the point nicely: "The Revolution was a beginning. The battle over its meaning can have no ending" (Lepore, 165).

Lincoln, King, and the other leaders I have been citing were not merely transmitters of culture; they were also agents whose power lay in forging new narratives from cultural ingots. In his Gettysburg Address, Lincoln told a story of the Civil War that not only drew on and resonated with historical and religious narratives, but also provided a new interpretation of the war, one that created possibilities for reconciliation (Wills 1992). It is not hard to imagine another president telling a completely different narrative, indeed stories that demonized the Rebels and demanded retribution were commonplace at the time. Similarly, Martin Luther King Jr.'s brilliant location of the story of the civil rights movement in the great Biblical and historical narratives of American culture was not inevitable. Other stories—black separatist accounts such as Malcolm X's, for example, or for that matter segregationist fantasies such as George Wallace's—could also be told. All of these figures drew on the narratives of their culture, but their interpretation was not wholly determined by it.

Once we allow for narrative agency in the telling, though, the question becomes: What stories work? What determines when a story will be taken up by a community, when it will shape common beliefs and attitudes, and when it will construct common interests?

First, clearly, material self-interest matters. The wealthy are more likely to accept stories in which the rich earn their money and the poor are lazy, and to resist those in which the rich are merely lucky while the poor are oppressed. Oil company executives are more likely to accept the story that climate change is a hoax and to reject stories about impending environmental disaster. Such alignment can be seen as a way to avoid cognitive dissonance (Festinger 1957): we act on our interests and then tell stories to justify our behavior. But even in these cases, it is interesting to note the need to justify. One never simply hears: "We are the dominant class, and we will exploit you because we can." At minimum, it seems, a story may be necessary to legitimize self-interest. But it cannot be only material self-interest that determines whether a story will capture the minds of a community, since many of our most strongly held interests are non-material and non-egoistic, as we explored in the last chapter. And even our material self-interest may not be obvious.

What else matters? Certainly, institutions that determine who gets to speak and who gets to be heard are important. The more we hear a story, the more likely it is that it will get in our heads (Cialdini 1993). Those in positions of power, therefore, have a considerable advantage. In the United States, notably, presidents are privileged in their access to the news media, and hence in their ability to tell the story (Entman 2004). And exposure to narrative depends on the community one belongs to. As has been well documented, the market for news has become ideologically segmented (Hamilton 2003). Viewers of *Fox News* get a very different mix of stories than readers of *The New York Times*.

Receptivity to narrative also depends on prior attitudes towards the storyteller. If we expect to hear music to our ears, we are more likely to tune in. Conversely, if we distrust the storyteller, we (metaphorically speaking) know how to put our fingers in our ears. As Samuel Popkin (1991) has argued, reliance on trusted experts is among the information shortcuts citizens use to interpret political events. Popkin analogizes this to firefighters relying on fire alarms rather than constantly looking out for fires: If there is something I need to pay attention to, the commentators I trust will alert me to the danger. Similarly, we know how to tune out those wolf-crying voices we have learned to distrust.

The persuasive power of a story also depends on the telling. Good stories are seductive, particularly if we don't know quite where the story is taking us. Sonya Cin, Mark Zanna and Geoffrey Fong suggest that narratives are less susceptible to being filtered when the point of the story is not immediately clear: "The counter-attitudinal message in a narrative may unfold so slowly, be so unexpected, be so subtle, that the reader fails to realize that the message falls within his or her latitude of rejection" (Cin, Zanna, and Fong 2008, 179). And once transported, it's too late to resist.

In large part, though, receptivity to narrative depends on the extent to which stories resonate with the stories we already have in mind, with the narratives of culture. Those who would use narrative to persuade tell tales that invoke and align with historical, religious, and ideological narratives. They ring true because they follow expected plot patterns, feature conventional characters, and repeat familiar meanings. The predilection for stories that fit existing cultural narratives can be so powerful that they all but construct themselves, which explains why urban legends propagate and persist. In literary terms, urban legends are synecdoches: specific instantiations whose form invokes more general narratives. They are stories that "must be true" because they so perfectly fit the story we expect. More commonly, though, there is some degree of narrative agency. Persuasive storytellers draw on the available cultural stock, but have considerable latitude both in choosing which cultural narratives to invoke and in shaping new narratives from them.

Martin Luther King's "Dream" speech, for example, draws its power from its skillful invocation of the great narratives of American culture, but freshly frames a story of the moment. From its opening echo of the Gettysburg Address to its recitation of the words of the Declaration of Independence, King's speech drew the audience into the American story, with its familiar march-towards-freedom plot, its conventional casting of America as the beacon of liberty, and its reassuring message of American exceptionalism. And throughout the speech Biblical phases triggered associations with the comforting religious narrative of Exodus, aligning the meaning of the moment with that most meaningful story. Through these references, King wove a new narrative with pitch-perfect harmonic resonance with the old.

## CONSTRUCTING COLLECTIVE GOODS

As I argued in Chapter 2, the need to construct the collective good is a great deal more common than we generally admit. Even classic public goods based on egoistic interests in security or economic gain usually involve an element of belief about the relationship between some choice and its consequences, and, therefore, require some construction to alert us to our "real" interest. And collective goods based on shared altruistic, ideological, patriotic, or other non-egoistic interests not only involve beliefs, but also, and fundamentally, require construction of those interests themselves. Moreover, construction must be coordinated so that the group shares a common interest.

### Egoistic Collective Goods

Classic examples of public goods depend on common egoistic interests. We generally assume that people will recognize their personal economic and security interests, and that, therefore, we need not consider how such interests arise or how they come to be shared. Common interests simply arise from common circumstances. But on closer inspection even classic public goods are often at least partially constructed.

In part, the need for construction arises because one's "true" interests are not always obvious. Interests in trade policy, for example, are usually assumed simply to reflect economic circumstance. But the relationship between a free trade agreement and one's job security is not always easy to discern; indeed, economic experts often differ on such matters. To understand the linkage requires both knowing what particular provisions (tariff schedules, rules of origin, etc.) pertain to one's particular sector of the economy and, often more difficult, projecting the effects of those provisions. If ever there were a case for remaining rationally ignorant, trade policy would be it. It follows that recognition of one's interests is not automatic and may depend on how the issue is framed (Hiscox 2006).

How, then, do individuals reach judgments about the effects of a trade agreement on their personal circumstances, and thereby recognize their self-interest with respect to supporting or opposing that agreement? As I have argued elsewhere (Mayer 1998), when the North American Free Trade Agreement (NAFTA) was voted on by Congress in 1993, for the vast majority of the public, beliefs about the economic effects of NAFTA, and therefore interests pro or con, depended less on analysis of facts than on the power of narrative frames. Opponents of NAFTA used several narratives to frame beliefs about the agreement. For example, union leaders portrayed NAFTA as a story of corporate greed and government collusion at the expense of workers. As a union worker wrote in the United Auto Workers magazine *Solidarity*,

"I see the destruction of America's working class.... [I]t is the destruction of the dreams, the expectations of each of us that our children will have a better life.... Those on the top are pushing the ones at the bottom right off the ladder." (Mayer, 266)

For workers, this story resonated with a worldview established by a meta-narrative in which corporations, and the politicians beholden to them, were always at war with workers.

Advocates of NAFTA did straightforwardly tout the economic benefits of NAFTA for business, but even within the business community, as lobbyists at the Business Roundtable sought to energize their membership, the pitch was a narrative about the epic battle between free trade and protectionism. Vice President Al Gore used the same frame effectively in a nationally televised debate with Ross Perot, who had made opposition to NAFTA a centerpiece of his third-party campaign for president the year before. Gore surprised Perot with the story of the 1930 Smoot–Hawley "Protection Bill." Holding up a picture of Smoot and Hawley, Gore said, "They raised tariffs and it was one of the principal causes...of the Great Depression" (Mayer 1998, 313).[10]

Like economic interests, security interests are usually assumed to need no construction, but that is not the case. We cannot always see where the danger lies, let alone know how best to confront it. A narrative may be needed to make security interests apparent, to awaken a community to a real danger over the horizon. Consider, for example, Winston Churchill's efforts to rouse England in the early days of World War II. Surely, one might think, the English needed no help in understanding the dangers posed by Hitler's Germany, but even after the Nazis invaded France, many in Britain still failed to see the threat. How did Churchill seek to persuade his public? Not alone by facts and logic, but also by dramatizing the situation through narrative. In his first speech to the House of Commons after becoming prime minister in 1940, Churchill gave a short speech calling his people to arms:

> [W]e are in the preliminary stage of one of the greatest battles in history.... We have before us an ordeal of the most grievous kind. We have before us many, many long months of struggle and of suffering. You ask, what is our policy? I will say: It is to wage war, by sea, land and air, with all our might and with all the strength that God can give us; to wage war against a monstrous tyranny, never surpassed in the dark and lamentable catalogue of human crime. That is our policy. You ask, what is our aim? I can answer in one word: victory; victory at all costs, victory in spite of all terror, victory, however long and hard the road may be; for without victory, there is no survival. Let that be realized; no survival for the British Empire, no survival for all that the British Empire has stood for, no survival for the urge and impulse of the ages, that mankind will move forward towards its goal. (Churchill 2003, 220)

Although Churchill tells only a small fragment of a story, his audience knew how to fill in the blanks. This is a tale that can only end in tragedy or triumph, defeat or victory, life or death. It is a tale intended to make clear the consequences of apathy, intended to inspire fear and awaken his people to the full implications of Hitler's menace: This is about survival! Clearly, the English people had a security interest in stopping Hitler. But note how Churchill frames the issue not so much about the personal survival of his listeners as about the fate of the British Empire, indeed even of the progress of mankind. To move his people, Churchill invoked the grand historical narrative of his people, a heroic myth of the British Empire as humanity's great civilizing force.

The role of narrative is also clear in George W. Bush's construction of US security interests after 9/11, but here, narrative did more than alert a people to its true interest. Images of the collapse of the World Trade Center Towers and the attack on the Pentagon were terrifyingly clear, but what they meant was not. As Americans struggled to comprehend the meaning of what had just happened, Bush used narrative to persuade the American public of his interpretation of its interests. In a speech to a Joint Session of Congress on September 20, a little more than a week after the attacks, President Bush framed the attacks as an "act of war against our country," unparalleled in American history "except for one Sunday in 1941." Bush cast the perpetrators as "the enemies of freedom" akin to the greatest villains in American history. "We have seen their kind before. They are the heirs of all the murderous ideologies of the 20th century. By sacrificing human life to serve their radical visions—by abandoning every value except the will to power—they follow in the path of fascism, and Nazism, and totalitarianism." And in words that echoed Churchill, he said,

> Great harm has been done to us. We have suffered great loss. And in our grief and anger we have found our mission and our moment. Freedom and fear are at war. The advance of human freedom—the great achievement of our time, and the great hope of every time—now depends on us. Our nation—this genera-tion —will lift a dark threat of violence from our people and our future. We will rally the world to this cause by our efforts, by our courage. We will not tire, we will not falter, and we will not fail. (Bush, 2001)

Bush's aim was to create a shared interest in fighting a "war on terror." To do that, he invited Americans to imagine their present circumstance through the familiar narratives available to them. The attacks were, sym-bolically, Pearl Harbor; our enemies, symbolically, Hitler, Stalin, and the litany of historical tyrants with whom America has historically fought. And note that Bush, like Churchill, told a story in which what was at stake was not the personal security of his citizens, but rather the fate of his country and its ideals. The question was whether America would stand once more for freedom against tyranny.

A similar case can be made for the role of narrative in constructing common egoistic interests in many other arenas in which we usually don't see the need for construction. Workers share an egoistic interest in higher wages and bet-ter working conditions, but it may not be obvious that they have an interest in forming a union. It is no coincidence that union organizing is replete with storytelling. Fishers share an egoistic interest in maximizing their yields, but it might not be obvious that they have a commons problem or an interest in establishing an institution for mutual restraint without some tragic narrative to make their predicament clear. Indeed, it is highly suggestive that it took a story, the parable of the "Tragedy of the Commons," for even academics to see the fundamental nature of the collective action problem involving commons.

The role of story is even more important when non-egoistic interests are the basis for collective goods, as I will shortly argue, but before turning to that however, it is worth noting that by using terms of moral significance for economic or security matters, storytellers seek to transform egoistic into non-egoistic interests. When America was attacked on 9/11, writes Brands, "This resurgence of evil presented an opportunity for Americans to resume their role as history's heroes..." thus "depicting the war on terror as not simply a moral imperative but a historical imperative as well" (Brands 2008, 278). For reasons that will become clearer in the next chapter, it seems that even when egoistic security interests are at stake, leaders commonly seek to construct a good based on non-egoistic interests.

## Non-Egoistic Collective Goods

Narrative construction of collective goods is even more important when those goods are based on altruism, ideology, or patriotic interests. In the previous chapter, I argued that when individuals are engrossed in a story of other, of ideas, or of the community, they come to have altruistic, ideological, or patriotic interests. Here I show that when a community is engrossed in a shared narrative of these kinds, its members can come to share such non-egoistic interests, and the furtherance of those interests becomes a collective good.

For those in the international human rights community, for example, narratives have been central to constructing common altruistic interests in the fate of others. In their research about transnational human rights activism, Keck and Sikkink (1998, 27) note, "In order to campaign on an issue it must be connected to a 'causal story' that establishes who bears responsibility or guilt." But why would so many around the world with no direct stake in the fate of those suffering human rights abuses be moved to take up their cause? Shared narrative appears to play a central role. Empathy for victims of human rights abuses depends on the power of their stories. Without stories we would not even know of the abuses; without identifying with the victims, we would not be moved to care. As the novelist J. K. Rowling has recounted about her time working at Amnesty International's office in London,

> There in my little office I read hastily scribbled letters smuggled out of totalitarian regimes by men and women who were risking imprisonment to inform the outside world what had happened to them. Amnesty mobilizes thousands of individuals who have never been tortured or imprisoned for their beliefs to act on behalf of those who have. The power of human empathy leading to collective action saves lives and frees prisoners. Ordinary people whose well-being and personal well-being are assured join together in huge numbers to save people they do not know and will never meet.... Unlike any other creature on this

planet, human beings can learn and understand without having experienced. They can think themselves into other people's places. (Rowling 2008)

In part, the power of the personal narratives of the kind Rowling describes lies in the universal appeal of such tragic tales. The genius of Amnesty International, the most important international human rights nongovernmental organization (NGO), was the way in which the organization used the stories of particular victims, "individuals with names, histories, and families," to build membership and to call attention to human rights issues (Keck and Sikkink 1998, 88). But translating empathy for particular individuals into an interest in the furtherance of "human rights" requires further construction, one that resonates with the worldviews and ethos of a larger community. As Mutua has argued, "The Universal Declaration of Human Rights (UDHR), the grandest of all human rights documents, endows the struggle between good and evil with historicity in which the defeat of the latter is only possible through human rights" (Mutua 2002, 15). Mutua argues that the appeal of the human rights construct for those in the West was the way in which it resonated with a narrative of Western exceptionalism, in which human rights advocates could cast themselves as the heroic rescuers of the oppressed in backward places.

Similarly, in the environmental arena, narratives appear to have been essential in constructing the collective good of environmental protection. Few people have a direct stake in preserving rainforests, protecting endangered species, or, indeed, minimizing climate change, yet many feel strongly about these issues. Interests in such environmental matters, therefore, must be constructed. For environmentalists of the 1960s, for example, Rachel Carson's *Silent Spring* (1962) was massively influential, a national bestseller and something of a bible for those in the environmental movement. As the preeminent biologist E. O. Wilson writes in his afterword to a recent edition of Carson's classic, it "delivered a galvanic jolt to public consciousness and, as a result, infused the environmental movement with new substance and meaning" (Wilson 2002, 357).

What is not widely recognized, however, is the extent to which Carson used narrative techniques. Carson begins her book not with a compilation of scientific evidence about the effect of pesticides and other chemicals, but rather with "A Fable for Tomorrow":

There was once a town in the heart of America where all life seemed to live in harmony with its surroundings... Then a strange blight crept over the area and everything began to change. Some evil spell had settled on the community.... Everywhere was the shadow of death....

There was a strange stillness.... The few birds seen anywhere were moribund; they trembled violently and could not fly. It was a spring without voices. On the mornings that had once throbbed with the dawn chorus of robins, catbirds, doves, jays, wrens, and scores of other bird voices there was now no sound; only silence lay over the fields and woods and marsh....

No witchcraft, no enemy action had silenced the rebirth of new life in this stricken world. The people had done it themselves. (Carson 1962, 1–3)

The story told in the first chapter is a simple tragedy. Once upon a time, all was well. Then comes a complicating action, a "strange blight" and "an evil spell," and the plot heads downward to death. Nature is the innocent victim; we (or those who create and use pesticides) are the villains.

What accounts for the popularity and the impact of *Silent Spring*? Certainly, it arrived at a moment in which evidence of environmental degradation was growing and in which new environmental groups were organizing. It is hard not to conclude, though, that Carson's skill as a storyteller made a difference. By organizing the mounting scientific evidence into a narrative, Carson's tragic tale breathed meaning into the situation. The story told in *Silent Spring* also had power because it resonated with a story already in the minds of many Americans, as part of a tradition of elegiac environmental narratives of American popular culture, narratives in which America's identity, in part, is bound up with the American wilderness. Thus, Carson's narrative helped to construct an ideology of environmentalism and to make environmental protection a collective good for the nascent environmentalist community.

And, in the civil rights movement, narrative certainly played a pivotal part in constructing civil rights as a collective good not only for African Americans but also for the wider community of Americans who joined their cause. The issue of voting rights demonstrates the point particularly clearly. As late as 1965, blacks in the South remained almost completely disenfranchised. Newly elected President Johnson was sympathetic to the cause, but there was little political reason for a Democratic president or legislators to act on the issue. To support voting rights in the South would have (and later did have) real costs to party support in that region, and there was not a particularly urgent reason for Northern whites to press the matter.

But on March 7, 1965, the story of what happened in the little town of Selma, Alabama, changed everything. That evening, the national networks broke into their regular programming with news from Selma. (The largest television audience, remarkably, was watching the movie *Judgment at Nuremberg*.) Television cameras had been positioned perfectly to capture the story. As peaceful marchers crossed the Edmund

Pettis Bridge at the edge of town, a line of Alabama state troopers—some with shields and gas masks, some on horseback—blocked their way. The marchers approached the line and stopped. The police ordered the marchers to disperse. The marchers silently held their ground. A few seconds later, the troopers waded into the marchers, beating then with clubs and firing tear gas canisters. As the marchers fled, police on horseback pursued and clubbed them.

What Americans saw that evening was stunning: innocent and unthreatening marchers met by masked and brutal police. For viewers, it was hard not to be moved by the dramatic scenes of good versus evil, hard to watch without identifying with the protesters and raging at the police, hard not to desire justice. Johnson seized the moment. Ten days after "Bloody Sunday," he spoke to a joint session of Congress:

> I speak tonight for the dignity of man and the destiny of democracy.... At times history and fate meet at a single time in a single place to shape a turning point in man's unending search for freedom. So it was at Lexington and Concord. So it was a century ago at Appomattox. So it was last week in Selma, Alabama....
>
> But rarely in any time does an issue lay bare the secret heart of America itself. Rarely are we met with a challenge, not to our growth or abundance, or our welfare or our security, but rather to the values and the purposes and the meaning of our beloved nation....
>
> There is no Negro problem. There is no Southern problem. There is no Northern problem. There is only an American problem....
>
> What happened in Selma is part of a far larger movement which reaches into every section and state of America. It is the effort of American Negroes to secure for themselves the full blessings of American life. Their cause must be our cause too. Because it's not just Negroes, but really it's all of us, who must overcome the crippling legacy of bigotry and injustice.
>
> And we shall overcome. (Waldman 2003, 195)

In his remarkable speech, Johnson located the story of Selma in the larger American story, an episode in the American historical narrative co-equal to Lexington, Concord, and Appomattox, and made passage of a voting rights act a shared patriotic interest. At stake was the fate of America itself.

In all of these cases, human rights, environmental protection, and civil rights, even trade policy and national security, storytelling leaders sought to define the collective good by providing the community with a story though which it could interpret its circumstance and establish its interests. Their stories had power in part because these storytellers had platforms from which to speak and credibility with their audiences, but also because they skillfully told a story that resonated with the grand narratives of culture already in the minds of their audiences.

## A NOTE ON THE "COLLECTIVE INTEREST"

Throughout this book, I have avoided the term "collective interest" in favor of "common" or "shared" interests, on the grounds that interests are held by individuals, not by groups. Whether and how one can think about the preferences of collectives is a central issue for the social sciences, of course. Normatively, as Arrow (1951) famously demonstrated, if individuals differ in their interests, it is logically impossible to aggregate from individual preferences to a common social preference without violating basic principles of consistency. In positive social science, the question of whether or not we can treat aggregates as if they were unitary actors with interests is more complicated. When there are significant differences within groups there is no particular reason to believe that the group as a whole will behave in ways that reveal a consistent set of interests, as the two-level games literature makes clear (Putnam 1988; Mayer 1992; Evans, Jacobson, and Putnam 1993; Mayer 2010). Nevertheless, in informal discourse and much academic literature alike, we commonly speak about the "national interest," the "concerns of the environmental community," and so forth, as if those collectives have coherent intentions.

One possibility, of course, is that this talk is simply in error, and that we should refrain from the fiction of treating collectives as actors with preferences. But it is also possible that our common language contains a profound insight: to the extent that shared narratives serve both to construct and to align the interests of its members, we can indeed say that there is a collective interest. In a sense, then, the "collective interest" is more than a convenient fiction; it can be a fact established by our fictions.

# CHAPTER 7

# Motivating Collective Action

*Satisfaction lies in the effort, not in the attainment.*
Mahatma Gandhi (1996, 41)

*A man dies when he refuses to stand up for that which is right. A man dies when he refuses to stand up for justice. A man dies when he refuses to take a stand for that which is true.*
Martin Luther King, Jr. (2012)

In the previous chapter, I discussed how political actors use narrative to construct collective goods. Yet, while a common conception of the good is necessary for collective action, it is hardly sufficient. Indeed, the existence of a collective good is usually taken as the starting point for analyzing the obstacles to collective action. In this chapter, I return to those obstacles, and to the question of how narrative might help to overcome them.

Recall that collective action to achieve a collective good requires first overcoming the temptation to free ride. Even if all aspire to the same end, each individual faces a temptation to allow others to bear the cost of contributing, marching, voting, protesting, and other forms of cooperating, in hopes of enjoying the outcome without bearing the costs of achieving it. As I described in Chapter 2, the essence of this problem can be modeled as a "social dilemma" game, the multi-party variant of the prisoner's dilemma. The prisoner's dilemma metaphor is surely the most widely used model in the social sciences, applied to analyze voting, interest group dynamics, legislative behavior, social movements, international relations, and more, all of which, of course, involve collective action problems. For all the attention paid to the social dilemma, however, the model does not capture all of the obstacles to collective action. Even if cooperation is somehow made more attractive than defection, collective action may founder on the twin problems of coordination and assurance. Whenever there is more than one way to cooperate, individuals need to coordinate if there is to be collective action. And if satisfaction from cooperating depends on participating in *collective* action, that is, on whether others also cooperate, each individual will need assurance that others will join in.

These are formidable obstacles. Despite them, though, humans do act collectively. We vote, we join, we volunteer, we contribute, we protest, we march, and we fight. The question is how we do it.

As I explored in Chapter 3, explaining collective action is a central preoccupation of modern social science. Theories of collective action correspond roughly to the rational choice, institutional behavior, and constructivist schools of thought. Each school contributes much to our understanding of how humans solve collective action problems, but for all its many insights, the literature is not fully satisfactory. Rational choice theories either require institutions it cannot explain or posit "expressive" or "identity" interests that must be constructed. Institutional theories do well with explaining coordination and assurance, but are not as successful in explaining cooperation in less institutionalized settings and can come close to squeezing out individual agency. Constructivism offers the promise of accounting for a fuller range of human motivation, but only rarely grapples fully with the problem of collective action. Framing theory is helpful in describing what might motivate collective action, but to demonstrate that frames matter is not to explain their genesis, their attraction, or their power. These shortcomings, I argued there, create an opening for a narrative theory of collective action.

The case for narrative depends on several prior arguments, each of which subsequent chapters explored. First is a recognition that we humans are, among other things, storytelling animals who use narrative to interpret our experience and imbue it with meaning, to establish our identity, and to script our actions. Second is a realization that as creatures constituted by narrative, we can be moved by narratives told to us by others, and that, therefore, stories can trigger emotions, alter beliefs, construct interests, and compel action. And, third is the insight that because stories can be shared (indeed, are designed to be shared), they can be held at once in many minds, thus aligning individual beliefs and interests, and constructing collective goods. I now turn to how narrative can overcome the three obstacles to collective action in pursuit of a collective good by compelling cooperation, facilitating coordination, and providing assurance.

## COMPELLING COOPERATION

A common interest in collective goods, whether the underlying interests are egoistic or non-egoistic, and almost no matter how passionately desired, is not sufficient to ensure cooperation in pursuit of the good. Unless enjoyment of some benefit can be made contingent on cooperating in pursuit of that good, free riding will still be a temptation.

Scholars have suggested many possible solutions to this problem, among them providing selective incentives sufficient to change individuals' material calculations, structuring repeated interactions so that the possibility of inducing future cooperation by others makes present cooperation the better choice, and empowering institutions to facilitate negotiation and enable mutual commitments. Certainly, these approaches can and do lead to cooperation under many circumstances, but they far from exhaust the possibilities. It is clear that those engaged in collective action often cooperate not because of selective incentives, not because of anticipated future benefits, and not because institutions compel them to do so, but because they enjoy expressive or identity benefits from the cooperative act itself—from voting, joining, giving, marching, or the many other forms that collective action takes. The question remains, however: What determines those benefits?

My core argument here is that an engrossing narrative can make participation in collective action a source of expressive or identity benefits, and thereby compel cooperation. When we are engrossed in a shared narrative about collective action in which we see ourselves as actors in a social drama, autobiography and history align. Playing our part in the collective narrative becomes an act of personal meaning and an expression of our identity.

Those who would move collective action seek to foster just such an apprehension. They attempt to engross their community in a dramatic narrative that defines the meaning of the moment, stirs passions, and awakens interests. They strive to foster a sense of urgency, depicting the moment as the turning point in the drama, the point at which triumph and tragedy hang in the balance and the outcome hinges on what choice the community makes. They seek to pull their audience onto the stage, transforming each person from an interested bystander to an actor in the social drama, an actor in history. And, they try to foster the apprehension that this moment in the social drama is also the crucible of each person's autobiographical narrative, a self-defining moment when they will be forced to answer the question: "What did you do when history called?"

## Engrossing the Community

Those who would move a community to action seek to narrativize the moment. Their goal is to engross the audience in a dramatic narrative that defines what is happening and what is at stake. That is why collective action is so often preceded by the rally, the locker room pep talk, the moment of prayer, or the stirring speech on the eve of battle. Often the stories are of injustice or of some impending tragedy designed to awaken the community to its interests, to remind it of its values, and to stir its passions.

Consider the problem faced by organizers of anti-globalization protests in the late 1990s and early 2000s. Given the complexity of the relationship between World Trade Organization (WTO), World Bank, and International Monetary Fund (IMF) policies and their actual consequences, and given the truly global scale of the collective action required to push back at the system, getting people out to march on the streets was quite a challenge. To move people to act first required a level of engrossment in narrative sufficient to really stir emotions. Beginning with the 1999 "Battle in Seattle," where protestors in the thousands took to the streets to protest against the WTO during a meeting of national trade ministers, virtually every major international economic summit for several years became an occasion for large-scale protests by activists opposed to the form that globalization was taking. Characteristically, before and during such summits, the community of activists would gather to affirm their commitment to the cause. And at those meetings, leaders told the stories of the movement.

Typical of these gatherings was a rally held on April 14, 2000, the eve of a protest march against the World Bank and the IMF in Washington, D.C. The International Forum on Globalization (IFG), an alliance of organizations in the anti-globalization movement, hosted what it called a "Teach-in on the IMF and the World Bank." Several hundred activists crowded into Founders Methodist Church, a venue with echoes of the civil rights movement for many of the older participants.

The president of the IFG (with the great political name of Jerry Mander) opened the proceedings, a panel of speakers addressing "Globalization's Triple Threat: WTO, IMF & the World Bank":

> These institutions have presided over a truly disastrous combination of results: environmental destruction on a nearly planetary scale, deliberate undermining of the ability of nations to be self-reliant for food or other key needs, deliberate promotion of debt dependency on banks, destruction of public institutions for public health, social services, education and many more, and the achievement of the greatest rate of growth of separation between the wealthy

and the poor within nations and among them, with growing poverty, hunger and landlessness, and an endless number of other effects you'll hear described today and tonight. (Mayer 2007, 17)

And they did. For 14 hours, speakers told tales of exploitation of workers, indigenous peoples, and the environment by corporations abetted by the "unholy Trinity" of the World Bank, the IMF, and the WTO. For those in the audience, it was a day of total immersion in the narratives of injustice intended not so much to persuade as to reinforce beliefs, stir emotions, and signal the portent of the moment.

Such narrative immersions are common in collective action. The pattern of the rally against globalization differed little from that of the 1963 civil rights rally that preceded King's "Dream" speech, or a Tea Party rally on the Mall nearly half a century later. In such moments, the grand narratives are also recounted (or invoked), a move that facilitates the community's receptivity to the particular story being told, as we discussed in the previous chapter. Moreover, by locating the immediate challenge in the grand narratives, storytellers *historicize* the present. Their message is that what is happening today is part of a larger story, an episode in our collective story, a story of historical significance. That is why civil rights leaders reference American and Biblical mythology when telling the civil rights story, and Tea Party leaders retell the legend of the original Tea Partiers who stood up to British tyranny.

### Creating Crisis: The Fierce Urgency of *Now*

Inertia is the enemy of collective action. Often, the challenge for those who would spur collective action is to overcome the tendency to wait rather than to act. For this reason, leaders commonly seek to foster a sense of crisis by making the present the turning point in the story, the moment that will determine whether it ends in triumph or tragedy. The sociologist and union organizer Marshall Ganz (2008) calls this the "story of now." As King (2000) wrote in his 1963 "Letter From a Birmingham Jail,"

> You may well ask: Why direct action? Why sit-ins, marches and so forth? Isn't negotiation a better path? You are quite right in calling for negotiation. Indeed this is the very purpose of direct action. Nonviolent direct action seeks to create such a *crisis* and foster such a tension that a community which has constantly refused to negotiate is forced to confront the issue. It seeks to so *dramatize* the issue that it can no longer be ignored. (Quoted in Gottlieb 2003, 179, author's italics)

And in his "I Have a Dream" speech, King sought to make now the pivotal moment when the plot will either continue inevitably to disaster or turn towards triumph.

> We have also come to this hallowed spot to remind America of the fierce urgency of now. This is no time to engage in the luxury of cooling off or to take the tranquilizing drug of gradualism. Now is the time to make real the promises of democracy. Now is the time to rise from the dark and desolate valley of segregation to the sunlit path of racial justice. Now is the time to lift our nation from the quicksands of racial injustice to the solid rock of brotherhood. Now is the time to make justice a reality for all of God's children. (Mintz 2002, 254)

The effort to make *now* the turning point is common. Consider, as another example, the ending of Rachel Carson's *Silent Spring*:

> We stand now where two roads diverge.... The road we have long been traveling is deceptively easy, a smooth superhighway on which we progress with great speed, but at its end lies disaster. The other fork of the road—the one "less traveled by"—offers our last, our only chance to reach a destination that assures the preservation of our earth. (Carson 1962, 300)

Echoing the familiar language of Robert Frost's poem, Carson frames this as the moment that will determine whether the story ends in "disaster" or "preservation of the earth."

It is important to note that those who tell the story of now are also telling a story of hope for the future, a story whose ending is not yet written and that might still end in triumph (Ganz 2008). "Let us not wallow in the valley of despair. I say to you today, my friends, that in spite of the difficulties and frustrations of the moment, I still have a dream," said King on the Mall as his pivoted to his most famous lines (Mintz 2002, 254). Without hope, anger can become despair.

## Enlisting the Audience: Making It *Our* Story

Those who would move collective action seek to pull their audience from their seats onto the stage, transforming them from interested by-standers to actors in an unfolding drama. In one way or another, they try to persuade their listeners that their action and, more specifically, their *collective action*, is what will determine how the story ends. The message is simple: This is *our* story to write.

Consider another of Churchill's stirring speeches in the early days of World War II. In June 1940, after the fall of France, England stood alone, and many counseled Churchill to make an accommodation with Hitler. Churchill would have none of it. On June 18, he spoke in the House of Commons:

> I expect that the Battle of Britain is about to begin. Upon this battle depends the survival of Christian civilisation. Upon it depends our own British life, and the long continuity of our institutions and our Empire. The whole fury and might of the enemy must very soon be turned on us. Hitler knows that he will have to break us in this island or lose the war. If *we* can stand up to him, all Europe may be freed and the life of the world may move forward into broad, sunlit uplands.
>
> But if we fail, then the whole world, including the United States, including all that we have known and cared for, will sink into the abyss of a new dark age made more sinister, and perhaps more protracted, by the lights of perverted science. Let us therefore brace ourselves to our duties, and so bear ourselves, that if the British Empire and its Commonwealth last for a thousand years, men will still say, this was their finest hour. (Toye 2013, 57)

Churchill not only sought to historicize the moment and to create a sense of crisis, but also sought to pull his audience onto the stage of history, to make them the actors in the story. He is telling them: What we choose today will tell the tale. We hold our fates in our hands. "If *we* can stand up to him," if *we* "brace ourselves . . . and bear ourselves," *our* story will end in triumph.

At the March on Washington in 1963, after describing his dream, King turned back to the collective action that could make it a reality, to the collective story of the participants in the movement.

> This is our hope. This is the faith with which I return to the South. With this faith *we* will be able to hew out of the mountain of despair a stone of hope. With this faith *we* will be able to transform the jangling discords of our nation into a beautiful symphony of brotherhood. With this faith *we* will be able to work together, to pray together, to struggle together, to go to jail together, to stand up for freedom together, knowing that *we* will be free one day (Mintz 2002, 257, author's italics)

We can see the same rhetorical move in many other cases of collective action. Consider the immense challenge facing environmental activists intent on mobilizing action on climate change. Few problems could present greater difficulty in convincing a community of its efficacy. One of the more effective environmental leaders is Bill McKibbon, the founder of 350. org. At a gathering billed as "Powershift 2010," McKibbon addressed a group of young environmental leaders. His challenge was not to persuade his audience of the importance of the cause, or even of the urgency of the moment, but to foster the belief that their actions could make a difference.

> Very few people can ever say that they are in the single most important place they could possibly be, doing the single most important thing they could possibly be doing. That's you, here, now.
>
> You are the movement that we need if we are going to win in the few years that we have. You have the skills now. You are making the connections. And there is no one else. It is you.... (McKibbon 2011)

Like many others who seek to move a community McKibbon was trying to pull his audience onto the stage of history.

## Offering Identity and Meaning: Aligning Autobiography and History

Finally, leaders seek to make acting in the collective drama a defining moment in personal self-narrative—because even if all are persuaded of the historical significance of what is at stake, of the urgency of the moment, of the possibilities for collective action, there will remain a temptation to free ride unless acting in the social drama is personally satisfying. That is why leaders seek to align history and autobiography. They invite all to imagine that when they tell the story of their lives they will have to answer the question: What did you do when history called?

Like so many human truths, this move is perfectly captured by Shakespeare (Ganz 2001). In *Henry V*, the king rallies his outnumbered troops as they face the French forces massing against them. To those who lamented their small numbers and their dismal prospects, Henry says:

> This story shall the good man teach his son;
> And Crispin Crispian[1] shall ne'er go by,
> From this day to the ending of the world,
> But we in it shall be remember'd;
> We few, we happy few, we band of brothers;
> For he to-day that sheds his blood with me
> Shall be my brother; be he ne'er so vile,
> This day shall gentle his condition:
> And gentlemen in England now a-bed
> Shall think themselves accursed they were not here,
> And hold their manhoods cheap whiles any speaks
> That fought with us upon Saint Crispin's day. (Shakespeare 2005, 175–6)

Henry is offering his troops the greatest of gifts, a life of meaning and a heroic identity—the gift of a great life story. Immortalized in story, they would forever be the ones whose biography would become part of history.

After Bloody Sunday, King came to Selma to lead another march. Unbeknownst to the marchers, however, King had agreed to wait for a federal judge to grant permission, and so, much to the marchers surprise, after once more crossing the Pettis Bridge, King halted for a prayer, then turned the group around and led them back to Brown Chapel, the staging site for the protests. Many were confused. Some questioned King's leadership. Tensions and frustrations were high. Outside, police patrolled on horseback and with dogs. The moment was fraught with danger, and there was a good chance that the group would disperse.

It was in that context that King spoke. As was his style he began slowly, and in the audio recording of the event one can hear grumbling in the background. But his speech gathered force as he headed towards its climax.

> Deep down in our non-violent creed is the conviction there are some things so dear, some things so precious, some things so eternally true that they are worth dying for. And if a man happens to be 36 years old, as I happen to be, and some great truth stands before the door of his life, some great opportunity to stand up for that which is right, [but] he's afraid his home will get burned, or he's afraid that he will lose his job, or he's afraid that he will get shot or get downed by state troopers, he may go and live until he is 80, but he's just as dead at 36 as he would be at 80, and the cessation of breathing in his life is merely the belated announcement of an earlier death of the spirit.
>
> A man dies when he refuses to stand up for that which is right. A man dies when he refuses to stand up for justice. A man dies when he refuses to take a stand for that which is true.
>
> But we're going to stand up right here amid horses. We're going to stand up right here in Alabama amid billy clubs. We're going to stand up right here in Alabama amid police dogs if they have them. We're going to stand up amidst tear gas. We're going to stand up against anything they can muster up, letting the world know that we are determined to be free. (King 2012)

Who, hearing this speech, could walk away? King is saying: Not only is this a dramatic moment in history, in the collective story, but also that this is a defining episode in your life story. He is offering meaning and identity. He is inviting all present to consider the story they will tell about what they did in that pivotal moment when in old age they look back on their lives. He is saying: If you do not take a stand now, you die, your story might as well end here. But, if you take a stand, you have a chance to be a part of history, a chance for a life story with meaning and purpose, a chance for salvation.[2]

King's rhetorical move is common. Consider the rhetoric of organizers at the anti-globalization march in Washington, D.C., in 2000. Faced with the same need to overcome the free rider problem, the organizers sought to make the choice to act a question of personal identity. Oronto Douglas, a human rights attorney from Nigeria, echoed King's words in Selma:

> When people remain silent, when you remain quiet, when the face of oppression is manifesting before your very eyes, then I say you are dead. But when you stand up to demand now, as we are requesting that you demand, I say you are alive. And you are protecting people thousands and thousands of years to come. People you do not know, have never met, people will stand up to say today in this historic moment there were people in the United States, people [from] around the world, who stood in Washington, against bullets, against batons, with pulpits, with drums, with dances, to demand that there should be change in this global casino. (Mayer 2007, 20)

Thus, by harnessing the power of narrative to engross us and stir our passions, to foster a sense of dramatic crisis, to transform us from audience to players on the stage of history, and, perhaps most importantly, to make participation in collective action the dramatic imperative of our autobiographical narrative, leaders overcome the free rider problem.

## COORDINATION AND ASSURANCE

Common interests in ends and common desires to participate in collective action are almost sufficient. Yet even when a community shares passionate interests and when participation in collective action to achieve them would be a satisfying expression of personal identity for its members, there may still be two related obstacles to collective action: the problems of *coordination* and *assurance*.

### Coordination

Whenever there is more than one way to cooperate, collective action requires that all agree on the form that action should take, as we discussed in Chapter 2. Sometimes, of course, coordination is unproblematic. Simple conventions solve many such problems: we drive on the right (in most of the world) without any problem. In more highly institutionalized settings, well-established rules coordinate behavior: legislators who want to pass a bill will know the sequence of required steps. In other circumstances, first movers may establish a norm, a standard, or some other institution to which others subsequently conform. And groups of individuals may negotiate a common approach. Even when there are no apparent conventions, situational characteristics may suggest themselves as "focal points" (Schelling 1960, 110).

With larger groups and less common occurrences, however, coordinating institutions are less likely to form and negotiated agreements more difficult to reach. Moreover, it may be impossible to specify *ex ante* every aspect of coordinated behavior. All may know to meet at a place and time for a protest march, but how protesters should conduct themselves as they march may be more difficult to coordinate by prior agreement. Under these circumstances, shared narratives can script coordinated behavior. Shared narratives can tell us *how* to behave collectively, how a revolution should be carried out, what a protestor does, how a society should respond to an insult. They enable participants to imagine the form collective action should take, and to anticipate how others will act. They orchestrate individual action into collective acts of meaning.

The narratives of culture provide possible scripts for community action. Myths, says Frye, carry with them *dromena*, a program for action (1998, 48). It is not surprising, therefore, that collective action often follows familiar narrative scripts. Drawing on Burke's "dramatistic" theory (Burke 1945), Turner argues that societies enact social dramas with classic narrative forms: "It can be seen that history repeats the deep myths of culture, generated in great social crises at turning points of change" (Turner 1974, 122). Father Miguel Hildalgo's ill-fated people's revolt at the outset of the Mexican Revolution, for example, took the form it did because it was experienced as a social drama in the form of a crusade, with Hidalgo and his indigenous followers marching beneath the banner of Our Lady of Guadeloupe against the Castilian oppressors.

Similarly, Walzer (1985) has argued that the Biblical story of Exodus continues to serve as the ante-type for contemporary movements. Because the story has been so "deeply etched into our political culture," it structures Western politics. Walzer quotes Davies (1982, 60):

> "We still believe, or many of us do, what Exodus first taught, or what it has commonly been taken to teach, about the meaning and possibility of politics and about its proper form:
>
> —first, that wherever you live, it is probably Egypt;

—second, that there is a better place, a world more attractive, a promised land;

—and third, that 'the way to the land is through the wilderness.' There is no way to get from here to there except by joining together and marching." (Walzer 1985, 149)

And it is not just that we think this way; our imagination structures our actions. "It isn't only the case that events fall, almost naturally, into an Exodus shape; we work actively to give them that shape," argues Walzer, "We complain about oppression; we hope...for deliverance; we join in covenants and constitutions; we aim at a new and better social order" (Walzer 1985, 134).[3] Tilly (1995; 2004; 2006) has argued that societies have "repertoires of collective action" that script their collective behaviors: "People learn to break windows in protest, attack pilloried prisoners, tear down dishonored houses, stage public marches, petition, hold formal meetings, organize special-interest associations" (1995, 26). The form of action reflects different cultural traditions. Since the 16th century, the French have erected barricades; Americans, it seems, march on Washington.[4] The existence of these patterns suggests, at minimum, that "participants in action attend to each other's assigned parts in the drama and to shared memories of similar events" (Tilly 2006, 27). These repertoires are not simply routines; they are enactments in which participants know their roles because they know how the story should go.

Note that many of these examples of collective action are themselves symbolic actions, designed not to accomplish a goal directly, but to play to a wider audience. Not surprisingly, the role of narrative in coordinating collective action is more pronounced for such symbolic collective action. Consider, as an example, the case of the Freedom Riders during the civil rights movement. The plan, as John Lewis recounts in his autobiography (Lewis and D'Orso 1998), was for an integrated group of civil rights activists to travel by bus from Washington, D.C., deeper and deeper into the South, ending in Mississippi, symbolically the belly of beast, challenging at every stop the segregated facilities of the Jim Crow South. All understood the potential for violence. But to succeed in dramatizing the injustice of the situation, every member of the team of riders had to follow the nonviolent tactics of the movement, had to understand the form of the story they were telling and the role it require them to play. As it happened, the violence was more than they bargained for, yet even after their bus was firebombed in Anniston, Alabama, the riders not only carried on with their journey, they stayed in role, calmly and bravely riding all the way to Mississippi, where they were arrested and sent to the notorious state prison farm at Parchman.

Similarly, awareness of the demands of social drama helped coordinate the protests in Selma. After Bloody Sunday, and after the aborted second march, King led a third march from Selma to Montgomery. For those who participated and for the nation that watched, the march was in many ways a classic social drama. A march has an inherently symbolic structure, with a beginning, a middle, and an end. It is an action by a symbolic army, a demonstration of coordinated power. This was a march out of Selma (Egypt), through the wilderness of rural Alabama, to Montgomery, which, if not quite the Promised Land, was relatively safe haven. By this point, through the lore of the movement, marchers knew what it meant to march and understood the symbolic structure of their collective action.

### Assurance

Finally, even when all have a deep drive to take part in collective action and all agree on the form cooperation should take, there may still be a problem of assurance. If enjoyment of expressive or identity benefits of cooperation depends on participating in *collective* action, those benefits will be contingent on the cooperation of others. Satisfaction from marching requires that others show up too. The essence of this situation is captured by Rousseau's stag hunt metaphor, in which if all are assured of the cooperation of others, then all will cooperate, yet if any believe that others will defect, defection becomes more attractive. The problem is, at heart, one of credible commitment. How can we be assured that others will do as they say? And how can we assure others that we will honor our commitments?

The problem of mutual assurance is, as we discussed in Chapter 2, a great deal more common than the literature has tended to acknowledge. From the basic social compact, to the stability of cooperative institutions, to all manner of circumstances in which mutual trust is essential to collective action, cooperation often depends on assurance that others will also cooperate. And in providing assurance narrative plays its most subtle role.

In part, narrative's power to assure is closely related to its role in human emotions. Frank (1988) has argued that emotions are commitment devices. For example, if we want to deter others from harming us by threatening retaliation, that threat may not be credible if, after they harmed us, there would be no advantage to retaliation, a fairly common dilemma. The emotion of anger, however, enables us, *ex ante*, to commit to retaliate even when, *ex post*, retaliation would not be rational. Similarly, the emotion of guilt prevents us from cheating when we are tempted to break our promises. Frank argues, further, that because we can recognize these emotions in others, we can know when other are committed. "The critical assumption behind the commitment model...is that people can make reasonable inferences about character traits in others" (Frank 1990, 87). Emotions make our commitments clear and credible.

Building on Frank, I argue that our emotional commitments depend on the way in which we can be bound by the narratives that capture our minds, and that the credibility of these commitments depends on our belief that others, like us, are also committed by narrative. First, as I discussed in Chapter 4, there is a very close relationship between narrative and affect. Not only are stories remarkably capable of triggering emotions, but the meaning of emotion itself is hard to disentangle from narrative emplotment. The emotion of guilt, for example, depends on narratives in which we fail to do the right thing, give in to temptation, abandon our comrades at moments of peril, cheat on the test, or otherwise act in ways that cast our character in a negative light. If we can tell a story in which the same behavior was justified—because we were compelled by circumstance or because others defected first (our favorite)—there is no guilt. Similarly, anger depends on a narrative in which the target of our anger is the villain, and we are the innocent victim. If the same act that angers us can be explained by a story in which it was justified, it is hard to stay angry. Our emotional commitments, therefore, depend on the meaning and stability of the narratives that underlie them.

Moreover, the credibility of emotions, and therefore, of their effectiveness as commitment devices, depends on our ability to recognize genuine emotion in others. As Frank explores, humans have a variety of ways of reading others' emotions, including our ability to interpret more-or-less involuntary physical manifestations. In part, though, the credibility of emotions depends on their appropriateness in some narrative. We distrust the emotional commitment of someone who appears to be angry for no reason. We want to know that that person is engrossed in a narrative in which anger is the necessary emotion.

The role of narrative in assurance is even more general than that of enabling emotional commitment, however. As Chapters 4 and 5 explored, the narrative of our lived experience can commit us to act as the plot demands of our character, commit us to act in ways that are intelligible, that are meaningful, and that maintain our identity. Our confidence in the commitments of others depends on what might be called the folk theory of narrative, our working understanding of the role of narrative in human behavior.[5] Because we believe that others, like ourselves, are creatures of narrative, believe that they, too, seek to maintain the integrity of their character, we are confident they will be held to their commitments by the dramatic imperatives of the narratives in which they are engrossed.

In situations requiring assurance, therefore, engrossment in the collective narrative commits us to cooperate, and demonstration of our engrossment makes our commitment credible to others. The sharing of stories that so often precedes collective action, therefore, serves not only to remind the community of what is at stake, but also to provide mutual assurance that all are committed to stay the course. This is what is happening when the crowd shouts its approval at the rally before the march, when the team cheers as it breaks the huddle before the game, when the troops cry out in response to the general's speech on the eve of battle. These are demonstrations that all are caught up in the collective drama of the moment.

For example, the success of non-violent resistance in the civil rights movement depended fundamentally on mutual assurance that all would respond to violence with non-violence. For the Freedom Riders, for example, if any retaliated, the story line would be muddied: almost certainly the media would report a riot provoked by the protesters rather than a morality tale in which the attackers were the clear villains. As the riders prepared for their journey they shared life stories, about how they came to be a freedom rider. Traveling during the initial uneventful legs, they sang together a song whose refrain was, "Hallelujah we are traveling down freedom's main line." For each to stay true to non-violence under this most trying circumstance required a belief that all others would stay true, a tremendous level of trust. And that trust was only possible because each knew that others' self-narrative made it impossible for them to do other than honor the path to which they were committed, because their character would not allow them to do anything other than to stay the course, regardless of consequence.

Or, to return one last time to the events in Selma of 1965, what John Lewis remembers of the eventual three-day march to Montgomery was that the "incredible sense of community—of communing—was overwhelming. We felt bonded to one another, with the people we passed, with the entire nation" (Lewis and D'Orso 1998, 344). What he is describing is the power of a shared narrative to assure a community. Immersed in a common narrative, all were committed to the collective action, and all could be deeply confident of the commitments of others.

## CONCLUSION

And so we return to August 1963 and the voice of Martin Luther King Jr. as he shared his dream with the thousands gathered before him at the Lincoln Memorial and the millions more who heard his words that day, and with the billions who still hear them today, and to the question of why his words had such power. The answer to this puzzle is one that we have been building towards in this book: by engrossing his listeners in story, he lifted them out of the cool calculus of self-interest to a passion for justice, enabled them to feel the dramatic potential of the moment both in the American story, and, crucially, in the story of their own lives, so that participation in the grand social drama became a personally meaningful and identity-affirming act.

This book has made strong claims about the role of narrative in cognition, affect, identity, and motive, about narrative's power to engross and persuade us, and, when shared, its ability to construct common interests, to compel cooperation, to coordinate behavior, and to assure us of our mutual commitment to collective action. Certainly collective action can and does happen for many others reasons. But there is a good reason why stories are so often present at the scene: narrative is powerful tool for those who would move collective action.

The utility of narrative for collective action has significant implications for the question of why we humans might have evolved a capacity for narrative. Certainly, the ability to act collectively conveys considerable evolutionary advantages. Other species have evolved quite complex forms of collectively coordinated behavior without the benefit of narrative. But narrative is a tool of enormous flexibility. It enables us to peer over the horizon, to anticipate dangers we cannot yet see, to hope for better futures, and to imagine what could be if we act collectively, or fail to do so. A species with such a capacity would be greatly advantaged in evolutionary competition.

Like many of our evolved traits—our taste for sugar, salt, and fat, for example—our narrative capacity is not an unalloyed good. The same tool that can be used to rally the people for a good cause can be used to provoke the mob for a bad. There are false prophets as well as true. Much harm as well as good has been done by the narratives of religion, ideology, and nationalism. And what may be a collective good for one group—winning a war, for example—is often a bad for another. Yet, it is also narrative that enables the best in us, that allows us to feel for others we do not know, to care about causes beyond ourselves, and to care for our community. And because the stories that move us can be held at once in many minds, our individual interests can align into a shared interest in a collective good. Most remarkably, though, narrative can solve the challenges posed by collective goods. When we are engrossed in a social drama, participation in collective action can become an essential element of our self-story, a necessary expression of our identity, and a satisfying act of meaning—thus overcoming the temptation to free ride. When there are many forms collective action might take, shared narrative helps choreograph our behavior. And when our community is caught up in a common story, we can be assured that others, like ourselves, will be committed to our roles in the collective drama. Perhaps, then, it should be no mystery why our narrative capacity is so close to the heart of what it means to be human, and why it is so central to our politics.

# NOTES

## CHAPTER 1

1. Often the terms public goods and collective goods are used interchangeably. I prefer to reserve the term "public good" for the narrower category of goods that satisfy the twin conditions of non-rivalry and non-exclusion, and to use the term collective good to encompass public goods as well as both common goods (common property resources) and club goods. Common goods are, like public goods, non-excludable, but they are rivalrous, in that consumption by one diminishes what is available for others to consume. Club goods are excludable but non-rivalrous.

2. Although some have sought to make a distinction between *narratives* and *stories*, I do not find the distinctions particularly useful in practice, given the breadth and fuzzy boundaries of the category, and therefore use the terms interchangeably.

## CHAPTER 2

1. The prisoner's dilemma game was first formalized by Merrill Flood and Melvin Tucker at RAND in the 1940s and given the "prisoners" interpretation by Albert Tucker in 1950 (see Tucker 2001).

## CHAPTER 3

1. Note that rational choice does not require that these interests be purely material or egoistic as long as they result in choices that satisfy the basic tenets of expected utility theory.

2. It is possible that altruistic interests, if sufficiently strong, might make cooperation the preferred strategy regardless of what others choose to do. This might be the case if individuals fully internalized the positive externalities of their actions (Elster 1989). On the other hand, if altruistic interests are somewhat weaker—individuals receive some benefits from others doing well, but the marginal altruistic benefits to any one individual of cooperating remain less than the cost—the altruistic objective is a public good.

3. There is an old story that captures the dynamic well. Steven Hawking begins his bestselling book, *A Brief History of Time* (1988; New York, Bantam Books), with one version: "A well-known scientist (some say it was Bertrand Russell) once gave a public lecture on astronomy. He described how the earth orbits around the sun and how the sun, in turn, orbits around the center of a vast collection of stars called our galaxy. At the end of the lecture, a little old lady at the back of the room got up and said: "What you have told us is rubbish. The world is really a flat plate supported on the back of a giant tortoise." The scientist gave a superior smile

before replying, 'What is the tortoise standing on?' 'You're very clever, young man, very clever,' said the old lady. 'But it's turtles all the way down!'" Geertz (1973, 28–29) tells essentially the same story, attributing it to an Indian philosopher.

4. On the other hand, some have argued that violations of rationality assumptions are not reduced by raising the stakes; see Tversky and Kahneman (1990).

5. In the ultimatum (or "take it or leave it") game, two parties may divide a fixed amount if they can agree on the division. One party makes an offer that the other party can reject or accept. If the amount available is $1, logic would suggest offering the bare minimum, say $.01, which the other party should, logically, accept, since it is better than nothing. In practice, extreme offers are rarely made for the good reason that they are not accepted. The dictator game has the same form except that one party simply decides what the division will be. Even then, when there is no possibility of rejection of even the tiniest amount, dictators don't offer the minimum.

## CHAPTER 4

1. To be clear, not every causal statement is a narrative. Statements of the form "carbon dioxide emissions lead to global warming" do not meet the minimum requirements of narrative.

2. Riessman draws on Labov (1982), who contends that a (fully formed) story has six structural elements: (1) an abstract, in which the substance of the narrative is summarized, "this is a story about..."; (2) an orientation, in which the initial context is established, "Once upon a time..."; (3) some complicating action, the sequence of events which create some dramatic tension; (4) a resolution, a final action in which the tension is resolved; (5) a coda, in which the perspective returns to the present; and (6) an evaluation, in which the significance of the action and the attitude of the narrative are clarified.

3. Other taxonomies are, of course, possible. Booker (2004), for example, argues that all stories fall into one of seven basic plots. Several of his plots are variants of the same basic plot structure in my taxonomy.

4. Some narratologists use the term *fabula* differently, as equivalent to *muthos*. See Bal (1985).

## CHAPTER 5

1. The casting of White, Johnson and others as innocents carried with it the subtext that homosexuals were complicit in their fate, a source of great frustration for many in the gay community. See Schellenberg, Keil, and Bern (1995). Attitudes about AIDS continue to be strongly influenced by attitudes towards homosexuality in many communities, with the consequence that AIDS carries a social stigma (Herek and Capitanio 1999).

2. See Hertzberg (2001) for a prescient take on the power of the war frame, and its perils.

3. The belief is demonstrably false, yet a CBS poll conducted in April 2010 found that 20 percent of Americans believed the "Birther" myth, as did 32 percent of Republicans. See S. Condon (2010), "Poll: "Birther" Myth Persists Among Tea Partiers, All Americans," retrieved from <http://www.cbsnews.com/8301-503544_162-20002539-503544.html>.

4. For an exploration of the question of the morality of patriotism, see Alasdair MacIntyre, "Is Patriotism a Virtue?" (2003). [COMP: Check Footnote Numbering]

# CHAPTER 6

1. Of course, by myth, I do not mean "untrue." Rather I mean it in the literary sense as a type of narrative. Indeed, as Frye (1982) notes, myths are often held to be the most true of stories, narratives that reveal what is "really real" about the human circumstances. We tend to associate mythology with primitive societies and to assume, therefore, that myths no longer operate in modern societies. In part this predisposition reflects the fact that it is harder to recognize as myth the narratives of one's own culture than it is to see them in the exotic other. But it is also because in the mobile, globalized world in which we now live, there is no single mythology to which all in a given society subscribe. (Of course, even the "primitive" societies in which mythology was first studied were a good deal more complex than early anthropologists imagined.) Nevertheless, though perhaps more dynamic and fragmented than in primitive cultures, mythic structures continue to be a central element of the culture, or cultures, to which we belong.

2. My use of the term *folk history* is similar to Bruner's (1990) use of the term *folk psychology*, by which he means the working theory of mind that people use to interpret the actions of others. Note that I am not focused here on the product of professional historians, or with the extent to which narrative should or should not enter their work. This is an interesting debate, however. One line of thought is that because both historian and audience share expectations about the form that significant human action must take, expectations determined by the possible narrative structures of culture, the act of producing a history inevitably becomes one of emplotment. As White puts it,

   > In the process of studying a given complex of events, [the historian] begins to perceive the *possible* story form that such events *may* figure. In his narrative account of how this set of events took on the shape which he perceives to inhere within it, he emplots his account as a story of a particular kind. The reader, in the process of following the historian's account of those events, gradually comes to realize that the story he is reading is of one kind rather than another: romance, tragedy, comedy, satire, epic, or what have you. And when he has perceived the class or type to which the story that he is reading belongs, he experiences the effect of having the events in the story explained to him. He has at this point not only successfully followed the story: he has grasped the point of it, *understood* it, as well. (2005, 225)

   A related debate concerns whether the narrative structure of history inheres in life, or whether it is only an artifact of the historian's creation. Mink argues that it is a mistake to think of the writing of history as the telling of the story that already exists: "There can in fact be no untold stories at all, just as there can be no unknown knowledge. There can be only past facts not yet described in a context of narrative form" (1978, 220). Carr, on the other hand, argues that we do indeed live stories before they are told, that because the subject of history is human agency and humans are ultimately enactors of narrative, there is a narrative dimension to human behavior: "It is not the case, as Mink seems to suggest, that we first live and act and then afterward, seated around the fire as it were, tell about what we have done, thereby creating something entirely new thanks to a new perspective" (1986, 150).

3. This narrative of the civil rights movement is not without contest. See Hall (2005).

4. For a liberal's take on this, see Lakoff (2004).

5. Narratives that foster collective identity generally also define who is "other," and may, indeed, cast them as villains. A consequence of strong in-group identification, useful in securing local public goods for a community, is that it may come at great expense to those "others" who do not have standing in the community's narrative. See, for example, Hardin (1995).

6. It is worth noting that the meaning of the Civil War is not entirely uncontested. In the South of my youth, it was still common to hear the war called "The War of Northern Aggression," in which the South and Southern way of life were the victims. Indeed, echoes of this framing still produce Confederate flag waving.

7. My definitions here are close to those of Geertz's: "A people's ethos is the tone, character, and quality of their life, its moral and aesthetic style and mood; it is the underlying attitude toward themselves and their world that life reflects. Their world-view is their picture of the way things, in sheer actuality are, their concept of nature, of self, of society" Geertz (1957, 421).

8. The Vietnam story is more contested than "Munich." For some in conservative circles, the tale is about weakness of resolve in staying the course. In this account, America would have won were it not for liberals and their allies in the media who undermined our efforts.

9. During the first year of Clinton's presidency, I served as a foreign policy aid to Bill Bradley, then-senator from New Jersey, and I had a front row seat for the debate about how to respond in Bosnia. I was struck then by how powerful the two narratives were in structuring not only the rhetoric but also the thinking of senators. It was clear that for some, Bosnia was "Munich," requiring that America meet the bully with force. For others, Bosnia was "Vietnam," implying that America had to resist the impulse to get involved.

10. Of course, the role of narrative in the politics of NAFTA was not confined to recognition (or construction) of economic self-interest. Many who engaged believed there was a threat to some other value. Although it was far from clear what impact, if any, NAFTA would have on the environment, for example, many in the environmental community opposed the agreement. For them, the story of NAFTA was another case of corporate evasion of regulation and outsourcing of pollution, an episode in the familiar tragic decline narrative that animated that community. Nor was it clear what impact NAFTA might have on illegal immigration or drug trafficking. Yet for right-wing opponents such as Pat Buchanan, NAFTA was another step towards erasing the border with Mexico, opening America to a flood of drugs and illegal immigrants, a story that resonated with the conservative narrative about the decline of America (Mayer 1998).

## CHAPTER 7

1. St. Crispin's Day is an old English holiday.

2. John Lewis's autobiography, *Walking With the Wind*, demonstrates alignment of autobiography with collective narrative (Lewis and D'Orso 1998). The American civil rights leader and now US representative will be forever the person who led the march in Selma and who acted with such courage and self-control as horse-backed police beat him on the Pettis Bridge. The Selma march is both the defining moment of his life and of the movement.

3. Note the implications of this perspective on the debate regarding the status of narrative for historians. If it is the case that humans enact narrative, then it is not just that historians impose a narrative form on events, but that events themselves already have a narrative form.

4. The prototype, of course was the 1963 March on Washington, at which King gave his "I Have a Dream" speech. That march, now etched in American consciousness, has become the template for all the other marches on Washington that followed, among them the Poor People's Campaign of 1968, the Million Man March of African American men in 1995, the Million Mom March against gun violence in 2000, and the Tea Party rally of 2009. So familiar is the march on Washington now that the comedians Jon Stewart and Stephen Colbert could stage a parody of the march in 2010 and draw tens of thousands.
5. The parallel is to Bruner's concept of "folk psychology," our working understanding of how others' think and behave (Bruner 1990).

# BIBLIOGRAPHY

Akerlof, George A., & Kranton, Rachel E. (2010). *Identity Economics: How Our Identities Shape Our Work, Wages, and Well-Being*. Princeton, NJ: Princeton University Press.

Akerlof, George A., & Shiller, Robert J. (2009). *Animal Spirits: How Human Psychology Drives the Economy, and Why It Matters for Global Capitalism*. Princeton, NJ: Princeton University Press.

Allison, Graham T. (1971). *Essence of Decision: Explaining the Cuban Missile Crisis*. Boston, MA: Little, Brown.

Anderson, Benedict R. O'G. (1983). *Imagined Communities: Reflections on the Origin and Spread of Nationalism*. London, UK: Verso.

Ariely, Dan. (2008). *Predictably Irrational: The Hidden Forces That Shape Our Decisions* (1st ed.). New York, NY: Harper.

Aristotle. (1947). Richard McKeon (Ed.). *Introduction to Aristotle*, New York, NY: The Modern Library.

Arrow, Kenneth Joseph. (1951). *Social Choice and Individual Values*. New York, NY: Wiley.

Associated Press. (October 19, 1987). Reagans offer Jessica 'big kiss'. Girl taken from well faces more surgery on foot. *Chicago Sun-Times*. Retrieved from http://www.highbeam.com/doc/1P2-3851002.html

Associated Press. (2009). Weis grants little boy's dying wish. September 29, 2005. Retrieved from http://sports.espn.go.com/ncf/news/story?id=2172623

Augustine, St. (2001). *The Confessions of St. Augustine*. London, UK: Frances Lincoln Publishers.

Axelrod, Robert M. (1984). *The Evolution of Cooperation*. New York, NY: Basic Books.

Bal, Mieke. (1985). *Narratology: Introduction to the Theory of Narrative*. Toronto, ON: University of Toronto Press.

Barthes, Roland. (1972). *Mythologies* (translated by Annette Lavers). New York, NY: Hill and Wang.

Bartlett, Frederic C. (1932). *Remembering: A Study in Experimental and Social Psychology*. Cambridge, UK: Cambridge University Press.

Bates, Robert. (1988). Contra contractarianism: Some reflections on the new institutionalism. *Politics & Society*, 16(2–3), 387–401.

Batson, Daniel C, & Powell, Adam A. (2003). Altruism and prosocial behavior. In Theodore Millon, Melvin J. Lerner & Irving B. Winer (Eds.), *Handbook of Psychology, Personality and Social Psychology* (Vol. 5, pp. 463–484). New York, NY: John Wiley & Sons.

Ben-Yehuda, Nachman. (1995). *The Masada Myth: Collective Memory and Mythmaking in Israel*. Madison, WI: University of Wisconsin Press.

Benford, Robert D. (2000). Framing processes and social movements: An overview and assessment. *Annual Review of Sociology*, 611–639.

Bennett, W. Lance. (1983). *News, the Politics of Illusion*. New York, NY: Longman.

Bennett, W. Lance. (1997). Storytelling in criminal trials: A model of social judgment. In Lewis P. Hinchman & Sandra K. Hinchman (Eds.), *Memory, Identity, Community: The Idea of Narrative in the Human Sciences* (pp. 72–103). Albany, NY: SUNY Press.

Bentley, Arthur Fisher. (1949). *The Process of Government: A Study of Social Pressures* (New ed.). Evanston, IL: Principia Press of Illinois.

Berger, Peter L., & Luckmann, Thomas. (1966). *The Social Construction of Reality: A Treatise in the Sociology of Knowledge* (1st ed.). Garden City, NY: Doubleday.

Bezgachina, Katerina. (2010). Habitat Bulgaria: Going against all odds. Retrieved from http://www.habitat.org/faces_places/hom/Hadziev.aspx#P0_0

Booker, Christopher. (2004). *The Seven Basic Plots: Why We Tell Stories*. London, UK; New York, NY: Continuum.

Bottici, Chiara. (2007). *A Philosophy of Political Myth*: New York, NY: Cambridge University Press.

Bower, Gordon H., & Cohen, Paul. R. (1982). Emotional influences in memory and thinking: Data and theory. In M.S. Clark and S.T. Fiske, (Eds.), *Affect and Cognition*. Hillsdale, NJ: Lawrence Erlbaum Associates.

Branch, Taylor. (1989). *Parting the Waters: America in the King Years, 1954–63*. New York, NY: Simon and Schuster.

Brands, Hal. (2008). *From Berlin to Baghdad: America's Search for Purpose in the Post-Cold War World*. Lexington, KY: University of Kentucky.

Brock, Timothy C., & Green, Melanie C. (2000). The role of transportation in the persuasiveness of public narratives. *Journal of Personality & Social Psychology*, 79(5), 701–721.

Bruner, Jerome S. (1986). *Actual Minds, Possible Worlds*. Cambridge, MA: Harvard University Press.

Bruner, Jerome S. (1990). *Acts of Meaning*. Cambridge, MA: Harvard University Press.

Bruner, Jerome S. (2004). Life as narrative. *Social Research: An International Quarterly*, 71(3), 691–710.

Burke, Kenneth. (1945). *A Grammar of Motives*. New York, NY: Prentice-Hall.

Burke, Kenneth, & Gusfield, Joseph R. (1989). *On Symbols and Society*. Chicago, IL: University of Chicago Press.

Burns, Jennifer. (2009). *Goddess of the Market: Ayn Rand and the American Right*. Oxford, UK; New York, NY: Oxford University Press.

Camerer, Colin F., & Fehr, Ernst. (2006). When does "economic man" dominate social behavior? *Science*, 311(5757), 47–52.

Campbell, Joseph. (1968). *The Hero with a Thousand Faces* (2nd ed.). Princeton, NJ: Princeton University Press.

Camus, Albert. (1955). *The Myth of Sisyphus, and Other Essays* ([1st American ed.). New York, NY: Knopf.

Camus, A. (1955). *The myth of Sisyphus*. New York: Knopf.

Carr, David. (1986). *Time, Narrative and History*. Bloomington: Indiana University Press.

Carr, David. (1997). Narrative and the real world: An argument for continuity. In Lewis P. Hinchman & Sandra K. Hinchman (Eds.), *Memory, Identity, Community: The Idea of Narrative in the Human Sciences* (pp. 7–25). Albany, NY: SUNY Press.

Carson, Rachel. (1962). *Silent Spring*. Boston, MA: Houghton MIfflin.

Chong, Dennis. (1991). *Collective Action and the Civil Rights Movement*. Chicago, IL: University of Chicago Press.

Churchill, Winston. (2003). *Never give in!: The best of Winston Churchill's speeches*. New York, NY: Hyperion.

Cialdini, Robert B. (1993). *Influence: the psychology of persuasion* (Rev. ed.). New York, NY: Morrow.

Cin, Sonya Dal, Zanna, Mark P., & Fong, Geoffrey T. (2008). Narrative persuasion and overcoming resistance. In Eric S. Knowles & Jay A. Linn (Eds.), *Resistance and Persuasion*. Rahway, NJ: Lawrence Erlbaum.

Coles, Robert. (1989). *The Call of Stories: Teaching and the Moral Imagination*. Boston, MA: Houghton Mifflin.

Condon, Stephanie. (2010). Poll: "Birther" myth persists among Tea Partiers, all Americans. Retrieved from http://www.cbsnews.com/8301-503544_162-20002539-503544.html

Condotta, Bob. (2005, September 26). Weis fulfills his promise, *The Seattle Times*.

Coser, Lewis A. (1992). Introduction. In Maurice Halbwachs, *On Collective Memory*. Chicago, IL: University of Chicago Press.

Csikszentmihalyi, Mihaly. (1997). *Creativity: Flow and the Psychology of Discovery and Invention*. New York, NY: Harper Perennial.

Dahl, Robert Alan. (1961). *Who Governs? Democracy and Power in an American City*. New Haven, CT: Yale University Press.

Davies, William David. (1982). *The Territoriality of Judaism*. Berkeley, CA: University of California.

de Sousa, Ronald. (1987). *The Rationality of Emotion*. Cambridge, MA: The MIT Press.

de Sousa, Ronald. (2013). Emotion. In Edward N. Zalta (Ed.) *The Stanford Encyclopedia of Philosophy*. http://plato.stanford.edu/archives/spr2013/entries/emotion/

Deacon, Terrence William. (1997). *The Symbolic Species: The Co-Evolution of Language and the Brain* (1st ed.). New York, NY: W.W. Norton.

Derrida, Jacques. (1976). *Of Grammatology* (1st American ed.). Baltimore, MD: Johns Hopkins University Press.

Deslandes, Jeanne. (2004). A philosophy of emoting. *Journal of Narrative Theory*, 34(3).

Dickinson, Emily (1998). *The Poems of Emily Dickinson* (Vol. 1). Cambridge, MA: Harvard University Press.

Dittmer, John. (1977). *Black Georgia in the Progressive Era, 1900–1920*. Urbana, IL: University of Illinois Press.

Donald, Merlin. (1991). *Origins of the Modern Mind: Three Stages in the Evolution of Culture and Cognition*. Cambridge, MA: Harvard University Press.

Downs, Anthony. (1957). *An Economic Theory of Democracy*. New York, NY: Harper.

Dunlop, Sally M, Wakefield, Melanie, & Kashima, Yoshihisa. (2010). Pathways to persuasion: cognitive and experiential responses to health-promoting mass media messages. *Communication Research*, 37(1), 133–164.

Dunn, Jennifer R., & Schweitzer, Maurice E. (2005). Feeling and believing: The influence of emotion on trust. *Journal of Personality & Social Psychology*, 88(5), 736.

Eagly, Alice H, & Chaiken, Shelly. (1993). *The Psychology of Attitudes*. Orlando, FL: Harcourt Brace Jovanovich College Publishers.

Eckel, Catherine C, & Grossman, Philip J. (1996). Altruism in anonymous dictator games. *Games and Economic Behavior*, 16, 181–191.

Eco, Umberto. (1984). *The Role of the Reader: Explorations in the Semiotics of Texts*. Bloomington, IN: Indiana University Press.

Edelman, Murray. (1964). *The Symbolic Uses of Politics*. Urbana, IL: University of Illinois Press.

Egan, Kieran. (1995). Narrative and Learning: A Voyage of Implications. In Hunter McEwan & Kieren Egan (Eds.), *Narrative in Teaching, Learning and Research* (pp. 116–126). New York, NY: Teachers College Press.

Elster, Jon. (1989). *The Cement of Society: A Study of Social Order*. Cambridge, New York, NY: Cambridge University Press.

Entman, R. M. (1993). Framing—Toward clarification of a fractured paradigm. *Journal of Communication, 43*(4), 51–58.

Entman, Robert M. (2003). *Projections of Power: Framing News, Public Opinion, and U.S. Foreign Policy*. Chicago, IL: University of Chicago Press.

Escalas, Jennifer Edson. (2004). Imagine yourself in the product. *Journal of Advertising, 33*(2), 37–48.

Evans, Peter B., Jacobson, Harold K., & Putnam, Robert D. (1993). *Double-Edged Diplomacy: International Bargaining and Domestic Politics*. Berkeley, CA: University of California Press.

Ezzy, Douglas. (1998). Theorizing narrative identity: Symbolic interactionism and hermeneutics. *The Sociological Quarterly, 39*(March), 239–252.

Farmer, Sarah Bennett. (1999). *Martyred Village: Commemorating the 1944 Massacre at Oradour-sur-Glane*. Berkeley, CA: University of California Press.

Fehr, Ernst, Fischbacher, Urs., & Gachter, Simon (2002). Strong reciprocity, human cooperation, and the enforcement of social norms. *Human Nature-An Interdisciplinary Biosocial Perspective, 13*(1), 1–25.

Fehr, Ernst, & Fischbacher, Urs. (2005). The Economics of Strong Reciprocity. In Herbert Gintis, Samuel Bowles, Robert Boyd & Ernst Fehr (Eds.), *Moral Sentiments and Material Interests: The Foundations of Cooperation in Economic Life* (pp. 151–193). Cambridge, MA: The MIT Press.

Feldman, Lauren, Maibach, Edward W., Roser-Renouf, Connie, & Leiserowitz, Anthony. (2012). Climate on cable the nature and impact of global warming coverage on Fox News, CNN, and MSNBC. *The International Journal of Press/Politics, 17*(1), 3–31.

Festinger, Leon. (1957). *A Theory of Cognitive Dissonance*. Evanston, IL: Row.

Finnemore, Martha, & Sikkink, Kathryn. (1998). International Norm Dynamics and Political Change. *International Organization, 52*(4), 887–917.

Flood, Christopher. *Political myth: a theoretical introduction*: New York, NY: Garland, 1996.

Forgas, Joseph P. (1995). Mood and judgment: The affect infusion model (AIM). *Psychological Bulletin, 117*(1), 39–66.

Forgas, Jospeh P. (2008). Affect and cognition. *Perspectives on Psychological Science, 3*(2), 94–101.

Forgas, Joseph P., & George, Jennifer M. (2001). Affective influences on judgments and behavior in organizations: An information processing perspective. *Organizational Behavior and Human Decision Processes, 86*(1), 3–34.

Foucault, Michel. (1972). *The Archaeology of Knowledge*. London, UK: Tavistock Publications.

Foucault, Michel. (1982). The subject and power. *Critical Inquiry, 8*(4), 777–795.

Frank, Robert H. (1988). *Passions within Reason: The Strategic Role of the Emotions* (1st ed.). New York, NY: Norton.

Frank, Robert H. (1990). A theory of moral sentiments. In Jane J. Mansbridge (Ed), *Beyond Self Interest*. Chicago: University of Chicago Press.

Frye, Northrop. (1982). *The Great Code: the Bible and Literature* (1st ed.). New York, NY: Harcourt Brace Jovanovich.

Gamson, William A. (1991). Commitment and agency in social movements. *Sociological Forum, 6*(1), 27–50.

Gamson, William A. (1992). *Talking Politics.* Cambridge, UK: Cambridge University Press.

Gandhi, Mahatma. (1996). *Mahatma Gandhi: Selected Political Writings.* Indianapolis, IN: Hackett Publishing.

Ganz, Marshall. (2001). The power of story in social movements. Unpublished paper prepared for the annual meeting of the American Sociological Association, Anaheim, CA, August 2001.

Ganz, Marshall. (2008). Why stories matter: The art and craft of social change. *Sojourners Magazine, 38*(3), 16–21.

Geertz, Clifford. (1957). Ethos, world view, and the analysis of sacred symbols. *The Antioch Review, 17*(4), 421–437.

Geertz, Clifford. (1973). *The Interpretation of Cultures: Selected Essays.* New York, NY: Basic Books.

Gergen, Kenneth J. (1999). *An Invitation to Social Construction.* London, UK; Thousand Oaks, CA: Sage.

Gerrig, Richard J. (1993). *Experiencing Narrative Worlds: On the Psychological Activities of Reading.* New Haven, CT: Yale University Press.

Girard, Bill (Producer). (2010). 9/12/09 DC Protest. Retrieved from http://www.teapartypatriots.tv/Videos.aspx?id=88dbc708-0c73-4f82-9f3a-31f283748086

Goffman, Erving. (1959). *The Presentation of Self in Everyday Life*: Doubleday Anchor.

Goffman, Erving. (1961). *Asylums: Essays on the Social Situation of Mental Patients and Other Inmates.* New York, NY: Doubleday.

Goffman, Erving. (1974). *Frame Analysis: An Essay on the Organization of Experience.* Cambridge, MA: Harvard University Press.

Goldner, Ellen J. (2001). Arguing with pictures: Race, class, and the formation of popular abolitionism through *Uncle Tom's Cabin. Journal of American & Comparative Cultures, 24*(1–2), 71–84. doi: 10.1111/j.1537-4726.2001.2401_71.x

Gottlieb, Robert S. (Ed.). (2003). *Liberating Faith: Religious Voices for Justice, Peace & Ecological Wisdom.* Lanham, MD: Rowman and Littlefield.

Graber, Doris A. (1984). *Processing the News: How People Tame the Information Tide.* New York, NY: Longman.

Green, Melanie. (2004). Storytelling in teaching. *Observer, 17*(4), 37–39

Gudmundsdottir, S. (1995). The Narrative Nature of Pedagogical Content Knowledge. In H. McEwan & K. Egan (Eds.), *Narrative in Teaching, Learning, and Research.* New York, NY: Teachers College Press, 24–38.

Guggenheim, Davis (Director). (2006). *An Inconvenient Truth* (motion picture). United States: Paramount Pictures.

Halbwachs, Maurice, & Coser, Lewis A. (1992). *On Collective Memory.* Chicago, IL: University of Chicago Press.

Hall, Jacquelyn Dowd. (2005). The long civil rights movement and the political uses of the past. *The Journal of American History, 91*(4), 1233–1263.

Hall, Peter A., & Taylor, Rosemary C. R. (1996). Political science and the three new institutionalisms. *Political Studies, XLIV*(6), 936–957.

Hamilton, James T. (2003). *All the News That's Fit to Sell: How the Market Transforms Information into News.* Princeton: NJ: Princeton University Press.

Hampton, Henry. (1986). Eyes on the Prize: America's Civil Rights Years, 1954–1965, Vol. 4: No Easy Walk (1962–66), PBS Video.

Hansen, Lene. (2006). *Security as Practice: Discourse Analysis and the Bosnian War*. New York, NY: Routledge.

Hardin, Garrett. (1968). The tragedy of the commons. *Science, 162*(3859), 1243–1248.

Hardin, Russell. (1982). *Collective Action*. Baltimore, MD: The Johns Hopkins University Press.

Hardin, Russell. (1995). *One For All: The Logic of Group Conflict*. Princeton, NJ: Princeton University Press.

Hardy, Barbara. (1968). Towards a poetics of fiction: An approach through narrative. *Novel, 2*, 5–14.

Hawking, S. W. (1988). *A Brief History of Time: From the Big Bang to Black Holes*. New York, NY: Bantam Books.

Heller, Anne Conover. (2009). *Ayn Rand and the World She Made* (1st ed.). New York, NY: Nan A. Talese/Doubleday.

Herek, G. M., & Capitanio, J. P. (1999). AIDS stigma and sexual prejudice. *American Behavioral Scientist, 42*(7), 1130–1147.

Hertzberg, Henrik. (2001, September 24, 2001). Tuesday, and after. *The New Yorker*.

Hinchman, Lewis P., & Hinchman, Sandra. (1997). *Memory, Identity, Community: The Idea of Narrative in the Human Sciences*. Albany, NY: State University of New York Press.

Hirschman, Albert O. (1982). *Shifting Involvements: Private Interest and Public Action*. Princeton, NJ: Princeton University Press.

Hobbes, Thomas. (1894). *Leviathan: or the Matter, Form and Power of a Commonwealth, Ecclesiastical and Civil*, London, UK: George Routledge and Sons.

Hume, David. (1978). *A Treatise of Human Nature*: Oxford, UK: Oxford University Press.

International Forum on Globalization (2000). On the IMF and the World Bank. Website. http://www.ifg.org/imf.html

Jackson, Philip W. (1995). On the place of narrative in teaching. In Hunter McEwan and Kieren Egan (Eds.), *Narrative in Teaching, Learning, and Research* (pp. 3–23). New York, NY: Teachers College Press.

Jewett, Robert, & Lawrence, John. (2002). *The Myth of the American Superhero*. Grand Rapids: W. B. Eerdermans.

Johnson, Dirk. (April 09, 1990). Ryan White Dies of AIDS at 18; His Struggle Helped Pierce Myths. *The New York Times*.

Johnson, Samuel (1785). *The Rambler*. (Vol. 1). London, UK: Harrison and Company.

Kahneman, Daniel, & Tversky, Amos (1979). Prospect theory—analysis of decision under risk. *Econometrica, 47*(2), 263–291.

Kahneman, Daniel. (2011). *Thinking, Fast and Slow* (1st ed.). New York, NY: Farrar, Straus and Giroux.

Kahneman, Daniel, Slovic, Paul, & Tversky, Amos. (1982). *Judgment under Uncertainty: Heuristics and Biases*. Cambridge, UK; New York, NY: Cambridge University Press.

Kalb, Marvin L., & Kalb, Deborah. (2011). *Haunting Legacy: Vietnam and the American Presidency from Ford to Obama*. Washington, D.C.: Brookings Institution Press.

Katzenstein, Peter J. (1996). *The Culture of National Security: Norms and Identity in World Politics*. New York, NY: Columbia University Press.

Keck, Margaret E., & Sikkink, Kathryn. (1998). *Activists Beyond Borders: Advocacy Networks in International Politics*. Ithaca, NY: Cornell University Press.

Keohane, Robert O. (1984). *After Hegemony: Cooperation and Discord in the World Political Economy*. Princeton, NJ: Princeton University Press.

Kermode, Frank. (2000). *The Sense of an Ending: Studies in the Theory of Fiction: With a New Epilogue*: Oxford, UK; New York, NY: Oxford University Press.

Khong, Yuen Foong. (1992). *Analogies at War: Korea, Munich, Dien Bien Phu, and the Vietnam Decisions of 1965*. Princeton, NJ: Princeton University Press.

Kidder, Tracy. (2003). *Mountains Beyond Mountains: The Quest of Dr. Paul Farmer, the Man Who Would Cure the World*. New York, NY: Random House.

King, Martin Luther, Jr. (2000). *Why We Can't Wait*. New York, NY: Signet Classic.

King, Martin Luther, Jr. (2012). Selma speeches of Martin Luther King. YouTube Video. http://www.youtube.com/watch?v=0On19DRA2fU

Kotre, John N. (1995). *White Gloves: How We Create Ourselves Through Memory*. New York, NY: Free Press.

Krasner, Stephen D. (1983). *International Regimes*. Ithaca, NY: Cornell University Press.

Krosnick, Jon A., & MacInnis, Bo. (2012). Trends in American public opinion on global warming policies between 2010 and 2012. Retrieved from http://woodsinstitute.stanford.edu.proxy.lib.duke.edu/sites/default/files/files/GW-Unilateral-Action-2008-2010.pdf

Krugman, Paul. (2008, April 11, 2008). Health care horror stories, *The New York Times*. Retrieved from http://www.nytimes.com/2008/04/11/opinion/11krugman.html

Lakoff, George. (1987). *Women, Fire, and Dangerous Things: What Categories Reveal About the Mind*. Chicago, IL: University of Chicago Press.

Lakoff, George, & Johnson, Mark. (1980). *Metaphors we live by*. Chicago, IL: University of Chicago Press.

Langer, Lilly M., Zimmerman, Rick S., Hendershot, Edward F., & Singh, Mimi. (1992). Effect of Magic Johnson's HIV status on HIV-related attitudes and behaviors of an STD clinic population. *AIDS Education and Prevention 4*(4), 295–307.

Lerner, Jennifer S., & Keltner, Dacher. (2000). Beyond valence: Toward a model of emotion-specific influences on judgement and choice. *Cognition & Emotion, 14*(4), 473–493.

Levi-Strauss, Claude. (1966). *The Savage Mind*. Chicago, IL: University of Chicago Press.

Levi, Margaret. (1997). *Consent, Dissent, and Patriotism*. Cambridge, UK; New York, NY: Cambridge University Press.

Lewis, John, & D'Orso, Michael. (1998). *Walking with the Wind*. New York, NY: Simon and Schuster.

Lischer, Richard. (1995). *The Preacher King: Martin Luther King, Jr. and the Word That Moved America*. New York, NY: Oxford University Press.

Luce, R. Duncan, & Raiffa, Howard. (1957). *Games and Decisions: Introduction and Critical Survey*. New York, NY: Wiley.

Lynch, Julie S., & Broek, Paul van den. (2007). Understanding the glue of narrative structure: Children's on- and off-line inferences about characters' goals. *Cognitive Development, 22*, 323–340.

MacIntyre, Alasdair. (1981). *After Virtue: a Study in Moral Theory* (American ed.). Notre Dame, IN: University of Notre Dame Press.

MacIntyre, Alasdair. (1984). Is patriotism a virtue? In Derek Metravers & Jonathan Pike (Eds.), *Debates in Contemporary Political Philosophy: An Anthology* (p. 286). New York, NY: Routledge.

MacIntyre, Alasdair. (1997). The virtues, the unity of human life and the concept of a tradition. In Lewis P. Hinchman & Sandra K. Hinchman (Eds.), *Memory, Identity, Community: The Idea of Narrative in the Human Sciences*. Albany, NY: SUNY Press.

Malinowski, Bronislaw. (1926). *Myth in Primitive Psychology*: New York, NY: W.W. Norton.

Mandler, Jean M., & Johnson, Nancy S. (1977). Remembrance of things parsed: Story structure and recall. *Cognitive Psychology, 9*(1), 111–151.

Marcus, G. E., Neuman, Russel, W., & MacKuen, Michael. (2000). *Affective Intelligence and Political Judgment*. Chicago, IL: University of Chicago Press.

Marshall, Sandra P. (1995). *Schemas in Problem Solving*. New York, NY: Cambridge University Press.

Mayer, Frederick. (2011). *Dramatizing Climate Change: The Role of Narrative in Environmental Collective Action*. Unpublished working paper.

Mayer, Frederick W. (1992). Managing domestic differences in international negotiation: The strategic use of internal side payments. *International Organization, 46*(Autumn), 793–818.

Mayer, Frederick W. (1998). *Interpreting NAFTA*. New York, NY: Columbia University Press.

Mayer, Frederick W. (2007). Constructing globalization: The role of narrative in the anti-globalization social movement. Working paper. Available at http://citation.allacademic.com//meta/p_mla_apa_research_citation/1/8/1/0/8/pages181080/p181080-1.php

Mayer, Frederick W. (2010). Multi-level games. In Enderlein, Henrik, Walti, Sonja, & Zurn, Michael (Eds.), *Handbook of Multi-Level Governance* (pp. 47–65). Cheltenham, UK; Northhampton, MA: Edward Elgar.

Mayer, Frederick W. (2012). Stories of climate change: Competing narratives, the media, and U.S. public opinion 2001–2010. Discussion Paper D-72, Joan Shorenstein Center on Press, Politics and Public Policy, Harvard University.

Mayer, John D. & Salovey, Peter. (1993). The intelligence of emotional intelligence. *Intelligence, 17*(4), 433–442.

McAdam, Doug, Tarrow, Sidney G., & Tilly, Charles. (2001). *Dynamics of Contention*. New York, NY: Cambridge University Press.

McAdams, Dan P. (1997). *The Stories We Live By: Personal Myths and the Making of Self*. New York, NY: Guilford Press.

McDonough, Frank. (2002). *Hitler, Chamberlain and Appeasement*. Cambridge, UK: Cambridge University Press.

McEwan, Hunter, & Egan, Kieran (Eds.). (1995). *Narrative in Teaching, Learning, and Research*. New York, NY: Teachers College Press.

McKibbon, Bill. (2011). Bill McKibbon speaking at Powershift 2011. YouTube Video. http://www.youtube.com/watch?v=CdF8wz4Jwm8

Mead, George Herbert. (1934). *Mind, Self and Society from the Standpoint of a Social Behaviorist*. Chicago, IL: University of Chicago Press.

Merk, Frederick, and Lois Bannister Merk. (1963). *Manifest Destiny and Mission in American History: A Reinterpretation*. Cambridge, MA: Harvard University Press.

Miall, D. S., & Kuiken, D. (2002). A feeling for fiction: Becoming what we behold. *Poetics, 30*, 221–241.

Michotte, Albert. (1963). *The Perception of Causality*. Oxford, UK: Basic Books.

Miller, Laura. (2010, Sunday, May 16). The girl who conquered the world: Why we can't get enough of Stieg Larsson's heroine hacker. *Salon*. Retrieved November 24, 2013 from http://www.salon.com/2010/05/16/girl_who_kicked_the_hornets_nest/

Miller, Peggy J. (1994). Narrative practices: Their role in sociologization and self-construction. In Ulric Neisser & Robyn Fivush (Eds.), *The Remembering*

*Self: Construction and Accuracy in the Self-Narrative* (pp. 158–179). Cambridge, UK; New York, NY: Cambridge University Press.

Miller, Peggy J., Potts, Randolph, Fung, Heidi, Hoogstra, Lisa, & Mintz, Judy. (1990). Narrative practices and the social construction of self in childhood. *American Ethnologist, 17*(2), 292–311.

Mink, Lewis. (2001). Narrative form as a cognitive instrument. In Geoffrey Roberts (Ed.), *The History and Narrative Reader* (pp. 211–220). London, UK; New York, NY: Routledge.

Mintz, S. (Ed.). (2002). *A History of Us: Sourcebook and Index: Documents That Shaped the American Nation.* Oxford, UK; New York, NY: Oxford University Press.

Mitchell, W. J. Thomas. (1981). *On Narrative.* Chicago, IL: University of Chicago Press.

Moe, Terry M. (1980). *The Organization of Interests: Incentives and the Internal Dynamics of Political Interest Groups.* Chicago, IL: University of Chicago Press.

Mousavizadeh, Nader. (1996). *The Black Book of Bosnia: The Consequences of Appeasement.* New York, NY: BasicBooks.

Mutua, Makau. (2002). *Human Rights: A Political and Cultural Critique.* Philadelphia, PA: University of Pennsylvania Press.

Nair, Rukmini Bhaya. (2002). *Narrative Gravity: Conversation, Cognition, Culture.* New Delhi, India: Oxford University Press.

Nielsen. (2007). Global consumers vote Al Gore, Oprah Winfrey and Kofi Annan most influential to champion global warming cause. Retrieved November 24, 2013 from http://nz.nielsen.com/news/GlobalWarming_Jul07.shtml

Nell, Victor. (1988). *Lost in a Book: The Psychology of Reading for Pleasure.* New Haven, CT: Yale University Press.

New York Times. (1976). 'Welfare queen' becomes issue in Reagan campaign: Hitting a nerve now. *New York Times (1923-Current file)*, p. 51. Retrieved from http://search.proquest.com/docview/122717098?accountid=10598

Noddings, Nel. (1984). *Caring: A Feminine Approach to Ethics and Moral Education.* Berkeley, CA, and Los Angeles, CA: University of California Press.

Noddings, Nel, & Witherell, Carol (Eds.). (1991). *Stories Lives Tell: Narrative and Dialogue in Education.* New York, NY: Teachers College Press.

North, Douglas C. (1990). *Institutions, Institutional Change and Economic Performance.* New York, NY: Cambridge University Press.

Olson, Mancur. (1965). *The Logic of Collective Action; Public Goods and the Theory of Groups.* Cambridge, MA: Harvard University Press.

Ong, Walter J. (1982). *Orality and Literacy: The Technologizing of the Word.* London, UK; New York, NY: Methuen.

Ortner, Sherry B. (1999a). *The Fate of "Culture:" Geertz and Beyond.* Berkeley, CA: California University Press.

Ortner, Sherry B. (1999b). *Life and Death on Mt. Everest: Sherpas and Himalayan Mountaineering.* Princeton, NJ: Princeton University Press.

Ostrom, Elinor. (1990). *Governing the Commons: the Evolution of Institutions for Collective Action.* Cambridge, UK; New York, NY: Cambridge University Press.

Ostrom, Elinor. (1998). A behavioral approach to the rational choice theory of collective action: Presidential address, American Political Science Association, 1997. *American Political Science Review*, 1–22.

Pagel, Mark D. (2012). *Wired for Culture: Origins of the Human Social Mind* (1st ed.). New York, NY: W.W. Norton.

Petty, Richard E, Cacioppo, John T, Strathman, Alan J, & Priester, Joseph R. (1994). To think or not to think: Exploring two routes of persuasion. In Sharon Shavitt & Timothy C. Brock (Eds.), *Persuasion: Psychological Insights and Perspectives* (pp. 113–147). Boston, MA: Allyn and Bacon.

Pinker, Steven. (1994). *The Language Instinct* (1st ed.). New York, NY: W. Morrow and Co.

Popkin, Samuel L. (1991). *The Reasoning Voter: Communication and Persuasion in Presidential Campaigns.* Chicago, IL: University of Chicago Press.

Prince, Gerald (1982). *Narratology: The Form and Functioning of Narrative.* Berlin, Germany: Mouton.

Propp, V. I. A., Pirkova-Jakobsonova, Svatava, & Scott, Laurence. (1958). *Morphology of the Folktale.* Bloomington, IN: Research Center, Indiana University.

Putnam, Robert. (1993). *Making Democracy Work: Civic Traditions in Modern Italy.* Princeton, NJ: Princeton University Press.

Putnam, Robert D. (1988). Diplomacy and domestic politics: The logic of two-level games. *International Organization, 42*(Summer), 427–460.

Raiffa, Howard. (1982). *The Art and Science of Negotiation.* Cambridge, MA: Belknap Press of Harvard University Press.

Reich, Robert B. (Ed.). (1990). *The Power of the Public Ideas.* Cambridge, MA: Harvard University Press.

Ricoeur, Paul. (1984). *Time and Narrative.* Chicago, IL: University of Chicago Press.

Ricoeur, Paul. (1991). Narrative identity. *Philosophy Today, 35*(1), 73.

Ricouer, Paul. (1995). *Oneself as Another.* Chicago, IL: University of Chicago Press.

Ridgel, Kayte (Producer). (2010). Atlanta— Nate Whigham on Voters Remorse & Racism Charges. Retrieved from http://www.teapartypatriots.tv/Videos.aspx?id=7428e8f3-dcf6-4ad7-953b-85b4686e22bb

Riessman, Catherine Kohler. (1993). *Narrative Analysis.* Newbury Park, CA: Sage Publications.

Riker, William H. (1984). The heresthetics of constitution-making: The presidency in 1787, with comments on determinism and rational choice. *The American Political Science Review, 78*(1), 1–16.

Rothstein, Bo. (2000). Trust, social dilemmas and collective memories. *Journal of Theoretical Politics, 12*(4), 477–501. doi: Doi 10.1177/0951692800012004007

Rousseau, Jean-Jacques. (1997). *The Social Contract and Other Later Political Writings* (Victor Gourevitch, Trans.): Cambridge, UK; New York, NY: Cambridge University Press.

Rowling, J. K. (2008). J. K. Rowling speaks at Harvard Commencement (Video). Retrieved from http://www.youtube.com/watch?v=wHGqp8lz36c

Rudrum, David. (2005). From narrative representation to narrative use: towards the limits of definition (Critical Essay). *Narrative, 13*(2), 195(110).

Ruggie, John. (1982). International regimes, transactions and change: Embedded liberalism in the postwar economic order. *International Organization, 36*, 379–415.

Ruggie, John Gerard. (1998). What makes the world hang together? Neo-utilitarianism and the social constructivist challenge. *International Organization, 52*(4), 855–885.

Rumelhart, David E. (1975). Notes on a schema for stories. In Daniel G. Bobrow & Allan Collins (Eds.), *Representing and Understanding* (pp. 211–235). New York, NY: Academic Press.

Rumelhart, David, & Ortony, Andrew. (1977). The representation of knowledge in memory. In R.C. Anderson, R. J. Spiro & W. E. Montague (Eds.), *Schooling and the Acquisition of Knowledge* (pp. 99–135). Hillsdale, NJ: Lawrence Erlbaum Associates.

Ryan, Marie-Laure. (2006). Semantics, pragmatics, and narrativity: A Response to David Rudrum. *Narrative, 14*(2), 188–196.

Said, Edward. (1979). *Orientalism.* New York, NY: Vintage.

Samuelson, Paul A. (1954). The pure theory of public expenditure. *The Review of Economics and Statistics, 36*(4), 387–389.

Sarbin, Theodore R. (2001). Embodiment and the narrative structure of emotional life. *Narrative Inquiry, 11,* 217–225.

Schattschneider, E. E. (1935). *Politics, Pressures and the Tariff; A Study of Free Private Enterprise in Pressure Politics, as Shown in the 1929–1930 Revision of the Tariff.* New York, NY: Prentice-Hall.

Schellenberg, E. Glenn, Keil, Janet Mantler, & Bem, Sandra Lipsitz. (1995). "Innocent victims" of AIDS: Identifying the subtext. *Journal of Applied Social Psychology, 25*(20), 1790–1800.

Schelling, Thomas C. (1960). *The Strategy of Conflict.* Cambridge, MA: Harvard University Press.

Schelling, Thomas C. (1984). *Choice and Consequence.* Cambridge, MA: Harvard University Press.

Schwartz, B. (1991). Social-change and collective memory—the democratization of George Washington. *American Sociological Review, 56*(2), 221–236.

Schwartz, Barry. (2000). *Abraham Lincoln and the Forge of National Memory.* Chicago, IL: University of Chicago Press.

Shakespeare, William. (1998). *As You Like It.* Oxford, UK: Oxford University Press.

Shakespeare, William. (2005). *King Henry V.* Cambridge, UK: Cambridge University Press.

Shiv, Baba, & Huber, Joel. (2000). The impact of anticipating satisfaction on consumer choice. *Journal of Consumer Research, 27,* 202–216.

Shleifer, Andrei. (2000). *Inefficient Markets: An Introduction to Behavioral Finance.* Oxford, UK; New York, NY: Oxford University Press.

Shore, Bradd. (1996). *Culture in Mind: Cognition, Culture and the Problem of Meaning.* Oxford, UK: Oxford University Press.

Simon, Herbert A. (1969). *The Sciences of the Artificial.* Cambridge, MA: MIT Press.

Skocpol, Theda, & Williamson, Vanessa. (2012). *The Tea Party and the Remaking of Republican Conservatism.* Oxford, UK; New York, NY: Oxford University Press.

Skyrms, Brian. (2004). *The Stag Hunt and the Evolution of Social Structure.* Cambridge, UK; New York, NY: Cambridge University Press.

Slotkin, Richard. (1973). *Regeneration through Violence: The Mythology of the American Frontier, 1600–1860* (1st ed.). Middletown, CT: Wesleyan University Press.

Smith, Adam. (2010). *The Theory of Moral Sentiments.* New York, NY: Penguin.

Snow, David A., & Benford, Robert D. (1988). Ideology, frame resonance, and participant mobilization. In B. Landermans, H. Kriesis & S. Tarrow (Eds.), *From Structure to Action: Comparing Social Movement Research Across Cultures. International Social Movement Research* (Vol. 1, pp. 197–217). Greenwich, CT: JAI Press.

Snow, David A., Benford, Robert D, Rochford, Jr., E. Burke, & Worden, Steven K. (1986). Frame alignment processes, micromobilization, and movement participation. *American Sociological Review, 51,* 464–481.

Snow, David A., & Benford, Robert D. (2000). Framing processes and social movements: An overview and assessment. *Annual Review of Sociology, 26,* 611–639.

Steinbruner, John D. (1974). *The Cybernetic Theory of Decision: New Dimensions Of Political Analysis.* Princeton, NJ: Princeton University Press.

Stone, Deborah A. (1988). *Policy Paradox and Political Reason.* HarperCollins.

Strange, Jeffrey J. (2002). How fictional tales wag real-world beliefs: models and mechanisms of narrative influence. In Melanie C. Green, Jeffrey J. Strange, & Timothy C. Brock (Eds.), *Narrative Impact: Social and Cognitive Foundations* (pp. 263–286). Mahwah, NJ: Lawrence Erlbaum.

Strauss, Claudia, & Quinn, Naomi. (1997). *A Cognitive Theory of Cultural Meaning.* Cambridge, U.K.; New York, NY: Cambridge University Press.

Swidler, Ann. (1986). Culture in action: Symbols and strategies. *American Sociological Review, 51*(2), 273–286.

Tarrow, Sidney G. (1994). *Power in Movement: Social Movements, Collective Action and Politics.* Cambridge, UK; New York, NY: Cambridge University Press.

Taylor, Charles. (1992). *Sources of the Self: The Making of the Modern Identity.* Cambridge, MA: Harvard University Press.

Taylor, Michael (1990). Cooperation and rationality: Notes on the collective action problem and its solution. In Karen Schweers Cook and Margaret Levi (Eds), *The Limits of Rationality* (pp. 222–240). Chicago, IL: University of Chicago Press.

Taylor, Shelley E. (1981). The interface of cognitive and social psychology. In John H. Harvey (Ed.), *Cognition, Social Behavior, and the Environment* (pp. 189–211). Hillsdale: Lawrence Erlbaum.

Tea Party Patriots website. (2010). Retrieved from http://teapartypatriots.ning.com/

Thaler, Richard. (1980). Toward a positive theory of consumer choice. *Journal of Economic Behavior & Organization, 1*(1), 39–60.

Thaler, Richard H., & Shefrin, H. M. (1981). An economic theory of self-control. *The Journal of Political Economy, 89*(2), 392–406.

Thaler, Richard H., & Sunstein, Cass R. (2009). *Nudge: Improving Decisions about Health, Wealth, And Happiness* (Rev. and expanded ed.). New York, NY: Penguin Books.

Thompson, Craig J. (1997). Interpreting consumers: A hermeneutical framework for deriving marketing insights from the texts of consumers' consumption stories. *Journal of Marketing Research,* 438–455.

Thorndyke, Perry W. (1977). Cognitive structures in comprehension and memory of narrative discourse. *Cognitive Psychology, 9*(1), 77–110.

Thucydides, & Crawley, Richard. (1933). *The History of the Peloponnesian War.* London, UK; New York, NJ: J. M. Dent & Sons; E. P. Dutton & co.

Tilly, Charles. (1995). Contentious repertoires in Great Britain. in M. Traugott, (Ed), *Repertoires and Cycles of Collective Action.* Durham, NC: Duke University Press.

Tilly, Charles. (2002). *Stories, Identities, and Political Change.* Lanham, MD: Rowman & Littlefield.

Tilly, Charles. (2004). *Social Movements.* Boulder, CO: Paradigm Publishers.

Tilly, Charles. (2006). *Regimes and Repertoires.* Chicago, IL: University of Chicago Press.

Tolkien, J. R. R. (1954). *The Lord of the Rings: Book Two: The Two Towers.* London: Allen & Unwin.

Toye, Richard. (2013). *The Roar of the Lion: The Untold Story of Churchill's World War II Speeches.* Oxford, UK: Oxford University Press.

Truman, David Bicknell. (1951). *The Governmental Process: Political Interests and Public Opinion* (1st ed.). New York, NY: Knopf.

Tuck, Richard. (2008). *Free Riding*. Cambridge, MA: Harvard University Press.

Tucker, Albert W. (2001). A two-person dilemma. In Eric Rasmussen (Ed.), *Readings in Games and Information* (pp. 7–8). Oxford, UK: Blackwell.

Turner, Victor. (1974). *Dramas, Fields, and Metaphors: Symbolic Action in Human Society*. Ithaca, NY: Cornell University Press.

Turner, Victor. (1980). Social dramas and stories about them. In W. J. Thomas Mitchell (Ed.), *On Narrative* (pp. 137–164). Chicago, IL: Chicago University Press.

Tversky, Amos, & Kahneman, Daniel. (1990). Rational choice and the framing of decisions. In Karen Schweers Cook & Margaret Levi (Eds.), *The Limits of Rationality* (pp. 60–89). Chicago, IL: Chicago University Press.

Von Neumann, John, & Morgenstern, Oskar. (1944). *Theory of Games and Economic Behavior*. Princeton: NJ: Princeton University Press.

Vygotsky, Lev. (1978). *Mind in Society: The Development of Higher Psychological Processes*. Cambridge, MA: Harvard University Press.

Vygotsky, Lev. (1986). *Thought and Language*. Cambridge, MA: MIT Press.

Waldman, M. (Ed.). (2003). *My Fellow Americans: The Most Important Speeches of America's Presidents, from George Washington to George W. Bush*. Napier, IL: Sourcebooks, Inc.

Walzer, Michael. (1985). *Exodus and Revolution*. New York, NY: Basic Books.

Wendt, Alexander. (1992). Anarchy is what states make of it: The social construction of power politics. *International Organization, 46*(2), 391–425.

Wendt, Alexander. (1999). *Social Theory of International Politics*. Cambridge; New York, NY: Cambridge University Press.

Wertsch, James V. (1985). *Vygotsky and the Social Formation of Mind*. Cambridge, MA: Harvard University Press.

Wertsch, James V. (1991). *Voices of the Mind: A Sociocultural Approach to Mediated Action*. Cambridge, MA: Harvard University Press.

Wertsch, James V. (1998). *Mind as Action*. New York, NY: Oxford University Press.

Wertsch, James V. (2002). *Voices of Collective Remembering*. Cambridge, UK; New York, NY: Cambridge University Press.

White, Hayden. (1980). The value of narrativity in the representation of reality. In W.J.T. Mitchell (Ed.), *On Narrative* (pp. 1–23). Chicago, IL: Chicago University Press.

White, Hayden. (2005). Introduction: Historical fiction, fictional history, and historical reality. *Rethinking History, 9*(2/3), 147–157.

Wilensky, Robert. (1982). Story grammars revisited. *Journal of Pragmatics, 6*(5–56), 423–432.

Williamson, Oliver. (1975). *Markets and Hierarchies*. New York, NY: Free Press.

Wills, Garry. (1992). *Lincoln at Gettysburg: The Words That Remade America*. New York, NY: Simon & Schuster.

Wilson, David Sloan. (2009). Evolutionary social constructivism. In Jonathan Gottschall & David Sloan Wilson (Eds.), *The Literary Animal: Evolution and the Nature of Narrative* (pp. 20–37). Chicago, IL: Northwestern University Press.

Wilson, E.O. (2002). *Afterward to Silent Spring: Fortieth Anniversary Edition*. Boston, MA: Houghton Mifflin.

Wilson, Major L. (1967). The concept of time and the political dialogue in the United States, 1828–48. *American Quarterly, 19*(4), 619–644.

Winter, Sidney G. (1989). Comments on Arrow and Lucas. In Hogarth, Robin M. & Reder, Melvin W. (Eds.), *Rational Choice: The Contrast between Economics and Psychology* (pp. 243–250). Chicago, IL: University of Chicago Press.

Winthrop, John. (1994). A model of Christian charity. In Miles Gunn (Ed.), *Early American Writing* (pp.108–112). New York, NY: Penguin.

Young, H. Peyton. (1998). *Individual Strategy and Social Structure: An Evolutionary Theory of Institutions*. Princeton, NJ: Princeton University Press.

Young, Oran R. (1994). *International Governance: Protecting the Environment in a Stateless Society*. Ithaca, NY: Cornell University Press.

Zaller, John. (1992). *The Nature and Origins of Mass Opinion*. Cambridge, UK; New York, NY: Cambridge University Press.

# INDEX

*Figures are indicated by "f" following page numbers.*

Charity websites, 89
Children: cultural transmission to, 112; self-awareness of, 74; telling stories, 65
Chong, Dennis, 33
Churchill, Winston, 117–118, 131
Cin, Sonya, 115
Civil rights movement, 1–2, 26–27, 33, 42, 104, 107, 108, 114, 122–123, 129, 136, 139. *See also* King, Martin Luther, Jr.
Civil War, 104, 107, 146n6. *See also* Lincoln, Abraham
Climate change, 26, 86, 91–92, 131
Club goods, 23, 143n2(Ch.1)
Cognition. *See* Psychological functions of narratives
Cognitive dissonance, 114
Coles, Robert, 79, 95
Collective action, 11–49; assurance problems. *See* Assurance problems; background to problem, 13–14; common interest in collective good, 4, 6, 8–9. *See also* Collective good, pursuit of; cooperation. *See* Cooperation; coordination. *See* Coordination; motivating, 125–141. *See also* Motivation from stories; narrative theory of, 2, 4, 8, 49; problems of, 13–29; pursuit of collective good, 4, 101–124. *See also* Collective good; scholarship on, 6; stories enabling, 8, 47–49, 140; theories of, 30–49. *See also* Theories of collective action
Collective good, pursuit of, 4, 101–124. *See also* Common goods; assurance and, 137–139; collective identity and, 106–107; coordination and, 134–137; culture and, 103–105; socialization, agency, and politics of public narrative, 111–116; worldviews and ethos, 108–110
Collective interest, 124
Collective memory, 41, 102, 112, 113
Comedy, 61
Commitment problem, 16, 23, 37, 137–138
Common goods, 4–5, 15–20. *See also* Public goods; club goods, 23;

constructing, 27–29, 116–124; distinguished from public goods, 19, 143n2(Ch.1); egoistic, 116–120
Common interest, 4, 6, 8–9, 14, 27–29, 124
Common property resources (CPRs), 18–19
Complicating action in stories, 55
Conservatism vs. liberalism, narratives of, 104. *See also* Tea Party
Constructivism. *See* Social constructivism
Contingent consent, 40
Cooperation, 5–6, 9, 24–27; aligning autobiography and history, 132–134; compelling, 127–134; coordinating, 24–27, 126; crisis and urgency of "now," 129–130; engrossment of community, 128–129; enlisting the audience, 130–132; evolution of, 34–36; Hobbes's view of, 14; identity and meaning, creation of, 132–134; as preferred strategy, 20, 126; prisoner's dilemma and, 5, 15–16, 16f; public goods and, 14, 19; repeated play and, 36, 48; social dilemma game and, 16–17, 17f; stag hunt and, 23, 24
Coordination, 5–6, 13, 24–27, 134–137; "battle of the sexes," 25–26, 26f; rational choice literature on, 33; repeated play and, 36; two-party coordination game, 24, 25f
Coser, Lewis, 113
Creation myths, 58, 59
Crisis and urgency of "now," 129–130
Critical theorists, 111–112
Csikszentmihalyi, Mihaly, 80
Culture, 103–105; framing and, 46–47; human evolution and, 65–66; material interests vs. cultural factors, 102; narrative forms and, 54–55, 58; power of narrative and role in society, 111–113; repertoires of collective action and, 136; schemas and, 42; shaping factor of, 45; shared narratives and, 44, 101, 106

Daniel Boone legend, 105
David and Goliath story, 61, 103
Deacon, Terrence, 65

Huber, Joel, 84
*Huckleberry Finn* (Twain), 81
Hume, David, 21

Icarus story, 57, 63
Identity and stories, 7, 95–96; collective
    identity and, 106–107, 146n5;
    creation of identity, 73–76, 132–134;
    narratives of others as templates for
    our self-stories, 95–96
Identity interests, 33–34
Ideological interests, 27, 29, 32,
    90–93, 110
"I Have a Dream" speech (King), 1–3, 42,
    116, 130, 131, 139–140, 147n4
Impure public goods, 18
*An Inconvenient Truth* (Gore film), 90–91
Institutionalism, 6, 30, 36–43, 126;
    behavioral institutionalism, 36, 38–
    43, 48; rational institutionalism, 36–
    38, 48; social constructivism, 43–47
Interdisciplinary approach, 4, 43
Interests, 28–29, 87–88. *See also*
    Common interest; altruistic interests,
    27, 29, 32, 88–90, 143n2(Ch.3);
    ideological interests, 27, 29, 32, 90–
    93; patriotic interests, 27, 29, 32, 93–
    94; special vs. general interests, 18
International Forum on Globalization,
    128–129
International human rights
    activism, 120
International Monetary Fund, 128

Jewett, Robert, 105
Johnson, Lyndon, 109, 122–123
Johnson, Magic, 84
Johnson, Mark, 44
Johnson, Samuel, 53
Jury trials, 85
Justification, 45, 68, 72–73, 77, 114, 138

Kahneman, Daniel, 39, 46
Kalb, Marvin & Deborah, 109
Katzenstein, Peter, 44
Keck, Margaret, 44, 46, 120
Khong, Yuen Foong, 109
Kidder, Tracy, 96
King, Martin Luther, Jr., 1–3, 10, 42, 114,
    116, 125, 129–134, 137, 139–140

Kosovo, 109
Kotre, John, 68, 74–75
Kranton, Rachel, 48

Lakoff, George, 43, 44
Langer, Suzanne, 68
Larsson, Stieg, 80
*Lassie*, emotional response to, 64, 81–82
Lepore, Jill, 114
Levi, Margaret, 40
Lévi-Strauss, Claude, 43
Lewis, John, 136, 139, 146n2
Liberalism vs. conservatism, narratives
    of, 104
Lincoln, Abraham, 82, 106, 113, 114
Lischer, Richard, 108
Local public goods, 18
Luckman, Thomas, 43
Lynch, Julie, 65

MacIntyre, Alasdair, 1, 7, 73, 75, 77, 78,
    101, 102
Malinowski, Bronislaw, 105–106
Manifest destiny, 108
Marcus, George, 73
Marshall, Sandra, 42
Marxism, 110, 111
Masada myth, 107
McAdams, Dan, 73
McClure, Jessica, 60, 88
McKibbon, Bill, 131–132
Mead, George Herbert, 43, 74
Mead, Margaret, 111, 112
Meaning: acts of, 76–78; creating,
    70–71, 132–134; memory as
    reconstruction of meaning
    making, 44–45; of stories, 63–64;
    symbolic meaning, 28, 44
Mediated action, 102
Memory. *See* Remembering
Metaphors, 44, 76
Michotte, Albert, 71
Mink, Lewis, 56, 68
Moe, Terry, 32
Moral judgments, 63, 71, 77
Morgenstern, Oskar, 14
Motivation from stories, 79–97,
    125–141; action and dramatic
    imperative, 96–97; compelling
    cooperation, 127–134; engrossment,

80–83. *See also* Engrossment of stories; identification and identity, 95–96; persuasion, 83–94. *See also* Persuasion

Munich capitulation of Chamberlain to Hitler, 108–109, 110

*Muthos,*55, 63

Mutua, Makau, 121

Myths, 57, 63, 65, 103, 105–107, 129, 135, 145*n*1

NAFTA (North American Free Trade Agreement), 117, 146*n*10

Nair, Rukmini Bhaya, 70

Narrative. *See* Stories and storytelling

Narrative code, 53–64; character, 61–63; meaning, 63–64; plot, 55–56; tragedy, 56–58; triumph, 58–61

Negotiation, 26

Nell, Victor, 80

New social movement literature, 46

9/11, response to, 36, 81, 85–86, 93, 118, 120

Noddings, Nel, 80

Non-egoistic interests, 31–32, 103, 120–124

Non-violent resistance, 139. *See also* Civil rights movement

North, Douglass, 40, 43

North American Free Trade Agreement (NAFTA), 117, 146*n*10

Notre Dame football story, 97

Obama, Barack, 86, 90–91, 144*n*3(Ch.1)

Olson, Mancur, 14, 17–18, 31, 32, 36

Ong, Walter, 63

Ortner, Sherry B., 113

Ostrom, Elinor, 37, 38

Parsons, Talcott, 36

Patriotic interests, 27, 29, 32, 93–94

Perot, Ross, 117

Persuasion, 28–29, 79, 83–94; attitudes, 68, 73, 83–84; beliefs, 28, 70, 84–87; interests, 87–94. *See also* Interests; values, 94–95

Peter Rabbit story, 56, 60, 63

Pinker, Steven, 65

Plot, 55–56; prototypes, 56–61

Popkin, Samuel L., 115

Prisoner's dilemma, 5, 15–16, 16*f*,34, 35, 125, 143*n*1(Ch.2)

Psychological functions of narratives, 7, 64–71; acting, 76–78; cognition, 66; creating meaning, 70–71; emotion, 45, 71–72; identity, 7, 72–76; remembering, 66–68; understanding, 68–70

Public goods. *See also* Common goods: asymmetric, 18; distinguished from common goods, 19, 143*n*2(Ch.1); impure, 18; local, 18; step goods, 19, 19*f*

Putnam, Robert, 37, 40

Rags-to-riches stories, 59

Rand, Ayn, 86

Rational choice, 6, 30, 31–36, 48, 126, 143*n*1(Ch.3)

Rational ignorance, theory of, 110

Rational institutionalism, 36–38, 48

Reagan, Ronald, 86, 88

Reciprocity, 40, 42, 48

Religion, 103, 108. *See also* Biblical stories

Remembering: autobiographical, 74–75, 104; collective memory, 41, 102, 112, 113; narrative and, 66–68; as reconstruction of meaning making, 44–45

Resurrection stories, 59–61, 60*f*

Revenge stories, 61

Ricoeur, Paul, 55, 69, 76

Riessman, Catherine Kohler, 55, 63

Rise and fall stories, 57–58, 58*f*

Rothstein, Bo, 41

Rousseau, Jean Jacques, 5, 13, 21, 23–24

Routines, scripting of, 39–40

Rowling, J. K., 120–121

Rudrum, David, 54

Ruggie, John, 44

Rumelhart, David, 67

Said, Edward, 111

Samuelson, Paul, 14

Sarbin, Theodore, 71, 73

Schelling, Thomas, 28, 64, 81

Schemas, 39, 41–42, 48, 67, 69, 110

Schumpeter, Joseph, 38

Schwartz, Barry, 113